WAYS TO THE SELF

Five Conversations

By

Murray Stein & Diane Stanley

CHIRON PUBLICATIONS • ASHEVILLE, NORTH CAROLINA

www.ChironPublications.com
Front cover and interior paintings by Diane Stanley

Interior and cover design by Danijela Mijailovic
Printed primarily in the United States of America.

ISBN 978-1-68503-490-0 paperback
ISBN 978-1-68503-491-7 hardcover
ISBN 978-1-68503-494-8 electronic
ISBN 978-1-68503-492-4 limited edition paperback
ISBN 978-1-68503-493-1 limited edition hardcover

Library of Congress Cataloging-in-Publication Data
Names: Stein, Murray, 1943- author. | Stanley, Diane (Artist) author.
Title: Ways to the self : five conversations / by Murray Stein & Diane
    Stanley.
Description: Asheville, North Carolina : Chiron Publications, [2024] | Includes
    bibliographical references. | Summary: "In this volume, Murray Stein and
    Diane Stanley explore, compare and contrast key features of the Buddhist
    view of Self liberation and the Jungian process of individuation. In Chapter
    One, they share experiences that opened a path to Self-knowledge in their own
    lives, including psychedelics, meditation, synchronicity, dreams and active
    imagination. The value of integrating transcendent experiences is explored
    in Chapter Two. In Chapter Three, they look at art work as soul-work, based
    on a series of twenty-four pictures from a Jungian analysis. What do such
    images, absent the specific dream content from which they arise, reveal about
    the direction of individuation? Chapter Four focuses on the tensions and
    difficulties of living in two worlds - the temporal and the timeless - as well as
    on the unconscious drive to bring them into synergy"-- Provided by publisher.
Identifiers: LCCN 2024034616 (print) | LCCN 2024034617 (ebook) | ISBN
    9781685034900 (paperback) | ISBN 9781685034917 (hardcover) | ISBN
    9781685034924 (limited edition paperback) | ISBN 9781685034931 (limited
    edition hardcover) | ISBN 9781685034948 (ebook)
Subjects: LCSH: Stein, Murray, 1943---Interviews. | Stanley, Diane (Artist)--
    Interviews. | Self. | Self--Religious aspects--Buddhism. | Jungian psychology.
    | Buddhism--Psychology.
Classification: LCC BF697 .S78 2024 (print) | LCC BF697 (ebook) | DDC 155.2-
    -dc23/eng/20241029
LC record available at https://lccn.loc.gov/2024034616
LC ebook record available at https://lccn.loc.gov/2024034617

Photo by Emilio Nasser

Table of Contents

Preface

In these conversations, which took place between February 2023 and February 2024, we initially set out to discuss the similarities and differences between the Buddhist notion of liberation and the Jungian concept of individuation. This topic was suggested by the conversation between C.G. Jung and Zen Master Shin'ichi Hisamatsu in 1958.[1] Their conversation ended in a seeming agreement, but afterwards Jung was troubled by some of his responses to Hisamatsu and realized there were possible misunderstandings about terminology and the perception of psychological vs. spiritual developments in the two positions. In our conversations, we sought to continue the dialogue where they left off. The following five conversations represent our attempt to pick up the threads that were left hanging and carry them further along. We do not claim to have found a final answer to the profound questions raised in the earlier conversation between Jung and Hisamatsu. Our hope is that we have filled in some of the empty spaces which were left open earlier due to lack of time then and because of Jung's frail state of health.

---

[1] "The Jung-Hisamatsu Conversation" in *The Couch and the Tree,* edited by A. Molino.

As our conversations progressed, we also found ourselves opening some other related topics, like the experience of Jungian psychoanalysis and the integration of conscious and unconscious dimensions of the psyche. The question of living in two worlds, the one temporal and the other non-temporal, became a central topic of interest.

The intent in making this little book was to keep the style conversational and informal. This is not an academic treatise. We did edit and recast the oral conversations somewhat for the sake of literary style and continuity of flow, but retaining the tone of cordiality and dialogical give-and-take was a high priority for us.

Murray Stein and Diane Stanley

CONVERSATION ONE

WAYS TO THE SELF

Psychedelics, Active Imagination, Dreams, and Jungian Psychoanalysis

Murray: To begin our conversation, Diane, I would like to pose a question for us to think about together. There's so much discussion these days about psychedelics as a method to treat certain types of mental illness, but also as a tool for gaining access to the archetypal Self and advancing individuation. Can you reflect with me on how your own experience with psychedelics might compare with active imagination and working with dreams as ways to the Self? A second related question will be: Do these methods have similar results with respect to what we call individuation in Jungian psychology? I don't know if we can answer these questions for certain, but we can compare our experiences and see what we come up with.

As far as I know, Jung never used any external means to stimulate his imagination or to make contact with the unconscious. He had a very strong imagination, was patient with its gradual unfolding, and was content to receive naturally the numinous experiences he needed for individuation as they came along in dreams and visions. He did see numinous experience as essential for individuation. It introduces the light of the Self to the conscious mind. But he did not use chemical methods. Now, we know that a lot of peoples around the world have used various types of psychedelics in their religious ceremonies to attain to the numinous, such as peyote among the Native Americans, Ayahuasca in South America, Soma in India, Beer in the ancient Eleusinian Mysteries, and so on. The use of psychedelics to induce religious experience is not a new thing. Since I haven't taken psychedelics myself, I can't compare active imagination and dreams with psychedelic experience. From your experience - you have done both - are they the same or importantly different?

Diane: Do psychedelics take you to individuation in the same way that active imagination can? Not in my experience. Nor are psychedelics exactly like dreams. If we say that dreams are the Royal Road to the unconscious, I would say psychedelics are a helicopter to the unconscious.

Murray: Very swift and direct, then, whereas dreams are more moderate and grounded in the recognizable.

Diane: Yes, a leap up and over. The Royal Road to the unconscious for me is dreams, and always has been. Interpreting dreams and extending them through active imagination proceeds gradually, in a developmental way, in my experience. On the other hand, psychedelics is more like a helicopter, a straight up, steep vertical ascent, dropping me into a place beyond my experience, especially as a 19-year-old. It left me in virgin enchanted territory for 10 hours, and then it was as if the helicopter picked me up and brought me straight back to the place we started, albeit with an unforgettable experience.

Murray: So, the link between ordinary consciousness and the visionary experience is not there. It's hard to make the connection between where the helicopter takes you and the place where you start from and where you end.

Diane: Yes, it was a leap between two realms. I saw a glimpse, a possibility of a dimension I never knew existed.

Murray: This seems to be a big difference, then, between the psychedelic trip and active imagination. In my experience, the path to a numinous experience is more gradual and grounded in everyday life and concerns.

Diane: That's the same in my experience of active imagination as well. In this first LSD trip, after about 10 hours, I "came down" and realized I couldn't remain in that state, but an impression remained and it gave me incentive to find a spiritual path. There had been a definite, though ineffable experience of something infinitely connected and alive. It was not only an incentive to find a spiritual path, but it gave me the push to do hard, sustained work towards increasing consciousness. I guess that's why LSD was called a "mind-expanding" drug!

Murray: So that experience motivated you to make a go on a journey that turned into an individuation journey. This might be a similarity in outcome between the two ways. My experiences in active imagination also had a strong effect on my future, but maybe not quite as dramatic.

Instead of a turnaround, for me it was a confirmation of a journey I was already on.

Diane: You received confirmation for a direction in which you were already going. That's such a boost, isn't it! For me, that first "trip" was beyond anything I could imagine. When I arrived in Boulder, Colorado at 19, I already had two years of college under my belt. But I didn't drink alcohol, tea, coffee, never smoked a cigarette, never took any drugs. I was a real Protestant Midwestern girl.

Murray: Weren't you afraid to take such a powerful drug?

Diane: I didn't know enough to be afraid! I arrived in Boulder like Alice in Wonderland. It was an amazing place in the '70's and immediately felt like home. It was in the middle of a progressive uprising and celebration. The Leary phrase, "drop out, tune in, turn on," had been in the air for some time. During my very first week in Boulder, I met a friend I thought I could trust. We didn't have an intimate relationship, but he was a good musician and played the guitar. That counted for a lot in those days! (laughter). He had considerable psychedelic experience, and was willing to share his expertise (laughter, both). He told me he had recently procured some Orange Sunshine—LSD from California considered to be the best—and offered to share it. So, we arranged a trip to begin in the late afternoon and finish around dawn. Acid is very, very intense so you need to be careful who you do it with, in what surroundings and circumstances. My friend arranged everything thoughtfully ahead of time, and it was a turning point in my life. Even though I was signed up to continue my studies at the University in the coming autumn, after the LSD trip I took a semester off and went to India.

Murray: Such a dramatic turn in your life, but why India? What was the connection? Why were psychedelics linked to India and not to Zurich? That's where I went, not because of psychedelics but by a number of synchronicities strung together. But I do know of several people who came to Zurich as a result of LSD trips.

Diane: People came to Zurich because of LSD trips? That's a new one! Had they read *Memories, Dreams, Reflections*? What did they hope to achieve in Zurich after LSD? It seems they would have gotten the opposite—a ruthless coming down to earth. I know Marie-Louise von Franz was very much against psychedelics. She asserted that they broke through into the unconscious like a robber.

Murray: This was Zurich in the '60's! Dr. von Franz was amused at what she called "soul tourists." She was tolerant and even accepted some into analysis. My friend, Nathan Schwartz, was one of them. She also saw that some of them had real gifts. And she was right. These soul tourists slowly landed on solid psychic ground, and some of them completed the training and became well-known teachers and analysts. Many of us studying in Zurich at that time were in our 20's. I was 26 years old when I arrived and 30 when I graduated. Nowadays, the average age of candidates-in-training is around 50! It's a very different scene.

Diane: That is certainly a different scene, from the 20s to 50s! For me, taking a break from university and running off to India was an odd choice. Why did I go? Why didn't I travel to Zurich or somewhere else? I had not the slightest interest in or knowledge of India when I grew up in Illinois. But neither had I heard of Jung or Zurich.

Murray: So, what brought India to mind? Why did you feel drawn to go to India? Did somebody say, "Go to India! They all live like this there!"

Diane: That's funny! No, nobody said that explicitly. After the LSD trip, USA seemed exceedingly materialistic and superficial, and the Christian church tired and dull. I guess India was in the air among the disillusioned youth! I had just met Swami Satchitananda at a Peace Fair in Boulder and liked his energy. The Beatles had gone to India, discovered meditation and wrote an album about their experience. Richard Alpert, of psychedelic fame, went to India and met his guru Neem Karoli Baba, came back glowing and with a new name, Baba Ram Das. His popular book, *Be Here Now*, was everywhere when I took my first LSD. India was in the Zeitgeist, and the Hindu Vedas made sense to me then—the idea of Atman / Brahman struck a chord. There was a buzz about all things Indian among the psychedelic initiates…

Murray: "Lucy in the Sky with Diamonds"! Remember that? When that song was popular, I made my discovery of Jung. It was 1968 in Washington, D.C. Again, not by psychedelics, even though they were very much in the air, but by a chance encounter with *Memories, Dreams,*

Reflections. That book had a kind of psychedelic effect on my mind. It opened me to a new world, like psychedelics did yours.

Diane: You had your own inner revolution. It sounds like it was quite a dramatic change of direction for you also. "Lucy in the Sky with Diamonds" was the Beatles banner song for LSD, but it applied to you as well! *A girl with kaleidoscope eyes....* That was me...idealistic and naïve. I'm pretty sure you weren't as naïve as I was. At 19, I thought if I went to India, I would find my "destined" guru as Ram Das had: a Sadhu wrapped in a blanket, unaffected by the world, needing nothing, teaching nothing except *all you need is love.* It seems ridiculous now, but I thought I would arrive in Shangri La, or at least meet people who had been to Shangri La. I wasn't a bit logical, reasonable or responsible. My parents certainly didn't appreciate it.

Murray: I'm sure they had no idea what was going on with you. Mine didn't either. "Jung? Who's that?" They thought I had gone over the edge when I took off for Zurich the next year.

Diane: After all, you were a graduate of Yale—not a vagabond hippy. I bet you didn't even have long hair! I can imagine your parents: "You want to do what?! Go where? Why?" It's funny looking back, isn't it.

Murray: Your helicopter ride with LSD took you to India, a place that you associated with the Atman, the Brahman. Mine took me to the Jung Institute in Zurich. Maybe not so different.

Diane: Yes, maybe not so different in the long, long run. We both wanted to make the unconscious conscious in our different ways. Though I could never have put it in those words. My first acid trip had no reference to India. Three particular things I remember all these years later. One was my initiation into William Blake. I had never seen Blake's art, and my friend opened up a huge colour book of his paintings and invited me to look at them. On LSD, you don't only look at pictures, you *enter* them in a timeless way. The image becomes alive. The second was classical music. At another point in the evening, my guide played Beethoven's 9th Symphony, which I had never heard. That was huge—an inner explosion of heart and soul.

Murray: Yes, I can imagine the impact! This presents an important difference between the LSD psychedelic experience and active imagination. LSD affects the neurons and the sense of perception. It affects sensation, whereas active imagination doesn't, or at least not to the same intensity. Active imagination is mentally induced; psychedelic experiences are chemically induced.

Diane: Even now, I remember the emotional explosion hearing Beethoven's 9th. And the third thing I remember about that night is being ushered outdoors. It was a summer evening; the stars were intensely bright and close. The campus of the University of Colorado is spacious and full of huge old trees and expansive lawns. It must have been the middle of the night because nobody was around. It was like seeing the living Universe for the first time. I didn't know that a Tree was a divine deity, always communicating. That's how it felt. The stars, myself—every living thing, interconnected in a shining web of mysterious meaning. Even the concrete of the sidewalk was alive and participating. Material and immaterial, everything shining, alive and indivisible. And who knew we live in a musical universe? The music of the spheres, each heavenly body humming its own chord, interwoven and in harmony. This was the experience.

Musical Universe

Murray: What an amazing description of the altered state! Truly mystical!

Diane: I suppose someone else might have used this psychedelic experience as a springboard to study art, music or even astronomy. But that wasn't my fate.

Murray: You use the word "fate." It's extraordinary that you would have picked up everything and just gone to India, a single young lady, 19, a girl from the Midwest. You didn't feel any risk or danger?

Diane: I should have felt risk and danger, but I didn't have enough sense. And I certainly didn't ask my parents their opinion. Actually, many young middle-class kids like myself were heading to India, wide-eyed and bushy-tailed. I met a few, and we travelled together.

Murray: Did you find what you were looking for?

Diane: Not on the initial trip. Not that first time.

Murray: It's similar with people who came to Zurich and didn't find what they were seeking.

Diane: Why do you think that was? Analysis was too difficult?

Murray: They were looking for a guru and transcendence. What they found was academic study and tedious analysis. Sometimes they could make the adjustment. And sometimes they just moved on to other destinations.

Diane: For me, the trip to India rather backfired. I didn't understand about the lack of hygiene in India and drank water straight from the tap. (A sin, for those who know about travelling in the East). I went from staying in ashrams in Northern India, to a houseboat in Kashmir with a few equally young and naïve college dropouts, friends my age. We managed to land in Sri Nagar just as the Indo-Pakistani war was heating up. We had to be rescued by locals. A kind and generous man (why did I never ask his name?) snuck us out in the middle of night in his own car. There was a real possibility we could have been kidnapped and taken as American hostages. This saintly Hindu man drove all night without headlights, so the car would not be spotted. Sometimes we could see soldiers in the dark, on each side of the road. He drove for well over 12 hours, stopping several times, over mountain passes, taking us six foolish kids all the way to the airport in Delhi. We flew back to the USA and all of us went back to college. I landed back at my parent's house in Illinois, with my tail between my legs. No guru, no enlightenment, and a belly full of parasites. "Mom, Dad, I promise I will finish university now!" I cried out for mercy.

Murray: So, going to India the first time was an episode in your life, but it had long term effects. I mean, you didn't stop traveling to the East.

Diane: Well, I finished university first.

Murray: What did you study?

Diane: Before the LSD trip, I had been a theatre and dance major. When I came back to Boulder, after my trip to India, I changed to Philosophy and World Religions. Much later I attended art school in Switzerland.

Murray: Would you say that kick-off experience on LSD had this result? When you considered what to study, it gave you a direction?

Diane: Yes, it gave me direction.

Murray: So, it was a powerful transformative experience, that first psychedelic trip. Did you take more psychedelics after that?

Diane: Of course, but mostly psilocybin (magic mushrooms). I told myself they were organic, not chemical, grew locally so therefore not "drugs." But actually, if I'm honest, I just kept trying to repeat that first experience on LSD, but never did. Finally, I realized I had to make gradual progress through work and study. I began sitting zazen regularly and studied at university, just dug in. What was your life like in Zurich?

Murray: I have always loved books and study. What was new for me was steady twice-a-week personal analysis. The emphasis was more on the analysis than on the academic study, and this was different from my earlier studies. I liked the combination, though. The inner world of the psyche as experience and the academic/bookish world of the psyche as learned from books came together in a miraculous way. It's like the alchemists moving between laboratory and library, back and forth, each feeding the flames of transformation. I imagine it's what the monks of the Middle Ages experienced as they moved from prayer to work during the day.

Diane: It sounds like the description of an alchemist's life. Enviable! I became more grounded after that first trip to India, sitting "zazen" every day and studying. Some people may be able to recreate their transcendent experiences on LSD, but I had to go right back to basics and deal with complexes, habits, and conditioning slowly, awkwardly.

Murray: Then the meditation took over? You left the helicopter behind and started walking.

Diane: Started crawling.

Murray: Ok, started crawling, slowly. So, you finished college and then what?

Diane: Yes, I finished college with honours and kept up a meditation practice throughout. There was a Buddhist community in Boulder, so I also had the advantage of some like-minded friends. I kept up ballet and modern dance throughout college, also back-packing in the mountains, and after graduation got my first full-time job. A pretty normal life for someone in her 20s, so perhaps I wasn't such a spiritual nut after all. I was serious about meditation practice though, and tried to do a few hours every day. It wasn't just me, there were others sitting zazen regularly like this.

Murray: A few hours every day?

Diane: Yes. We would do longer sessions once a month. I started doing meditation retreats as well, when I had time, going into the mountains and staying alone in a hut. Again, I wasn't the only one doing this. Looking back, I must have really wanted to connect with that *reality* again, which I had experienced on LSD, but in a sustainable way.

Murray: That *reality?*

Diane: The experience of interconnectedness, luminosity. I tried many times to helicopter back into that experience with psychedelics, but it didn't work. So, you see, it wasn't for lack of trying a quicker, lazier method! I just personally had no choice but to go about it slowly and steadily from where I was, a rank beginner.

Murray: But did the psychedelic experiences help or hinder your spiritual path?

Diane: The first time was very helpful. It opened *the doors of perception*, as Aldous Huxley coined the phrase. Surprise!

Solid consensus reality isn't actually so solid. But after the first few trips, psychedelics were not helpful. I stopped taking psychedelics because they were draining my energy. I knew intuitively that it wasn't the way forward anymore.

Murray: You had to find another way to advance your individuation.

Diane: You are correct, but I wouldn't have thought of it consciously. Confession—I did experience one final LSD trip, one more throw of the dice before I gave it up for good. I was around 23, had finished college and was in my first job. Again, a friend gave me a pure hit of LSD (as we used to call it), and off I went by myself into the mountains. I knew the mountain area around Boulder well because of hiking and backpacking with friends. On this occasion, I went alone and found an isolated spot on a high meadow. This was at 6 a.m. on a warm morning in late summer. It takes about 30 minutes for LSD to "come on" so I just lay down, relaxed and kind of fell asleep in the grass. When I woke, I was in another world, full of strands of light penetrating everything. Seeing a plant pushing up through the soil, the sun rising, birds beginning to wake and sing. The luminous fabric that connects all of the natural world. Indivisible, with me included. I think that was the first time I experienced compassion, not only for the living world, but for myself as well.

Murray: Compassion?

Diane: Yes, I felt compassion. Perhaps love is a better word because it was so natural. It's like you see yourself from two vantage points: your young self with all its frailties, efforts, uncertainty. Simultaneously you see your life from the viewpoint of the "hand high above your head." This greater *presence* is seeing you, understanding your need to grow and unfold, just like the plants and trees. That made me feel compassion. Love is patient and timeless, so is the Tao.

Murray: It's interesting that this psychedelic experience brings more than a change in perception. It has a strong emotional component. It brings a feeling, compassion. Active imagination can deliver something quite similar. That was my experience, the realization that "love never fails," as St. Paul says. Dante's last great vision was similar too: becoming one with "the love that moves the sun and all the other stars."

Diane: "Love never fails…" That's powerful. Did it begin as a flash and gradually become more stable? It sounds like a religious experience. Perhaps it was dormant in you, due to your upbringing, and active imagination let it unfold?

Murray: It was a time of crisis in my life. I was hit by a strong wind of doubt about the sustainability of love over the course of time. You know, as relationships age, love changes, and my sudden paroxysm of fear was that it would evaporate, just disappear, poof! So, I did an active imagination with that question. I have a stable inner space where I can take such questions and work with them. When I was there for a while an impulse led me to look upward into the heavens. I "saw" Jesus Christ in the skies, and the thought came to me – it was more than a thought, it was a revelation – that in Christ time and eternity are fused permanently, and that this signifies that "love never fails" because the timebound experience of love is joined to the eternal source of love, so it can never vanish or be extinguished. It is an eternal flame. I can't tell you what a sense of relief this gave me. It made me a true believer. It was like Dante's experience. Since then, I have had no doubt that love can ever fail, and I have to say that it also gave me a whole new take on what it means to be a Christian. It brought a new consciousness for me.

Diane: That revelation sounds more grounded and long-enduring than a vision on LSD. It became integrated into your character and grew stronger over time. That psychedelic experience in the mountains also took me to a different level, a different consciousness. After that, I didn't need to do psychedelics again.

Murray: What kind of consciousness was that? Did your ego disappear in that experience on the mountain?

Diane: Ego-consciousness was still there. That experience was just expanded awareness, ego-consciousness more subtle and in harmony with nature perhaps, but definitely still present.

Murray: In some mystical experiences, the ego seems to disappear, as for instance in the Zen Ox-Herding Pictures. In Picture number 8, the Enzo, there is no subject and no object, just a circle. This is achieved in Zen practice sometimes by the meditator and is considered the moment of enlightenment. Beyond space, beyond time – pure empty consciousness, the empty mirror. Can you say something about this from your experience with psychedelics and meditation?

Diane: Well, this is an interesting point. In my experience, psychedelics and meditation are different. Back in the day, LSD was referred to as "a trip" or "tripping." It's the ego-consciousness going on a journey, or trip, through various vivid, heightened phenomena and perceptions. Whereas, meditation is stripping away, uncovering. I can only speak for myself, but I wouldn't call any psychedelic experience "satori" (as indicated by the 8th Ox-herding picture).

Murray: Can you explain that?

Diane: I will give you an example. About nine years after the mountain experience, I was doing a spiritual practice of purification. I owned up to myself that I needed to correct some inappropriate actions I had taken—as we do when we're young and foolish! I had the good fortune at this time of being in communication with an eminent meditation master. After I explained my quandary and requested instruction, he suggested a particular practice using confession and a purification deity. I did it intensely for a few months, about eight hours a day. One night a short time after I went to bed, I experienced an essence powerfully shooting up from my heart through the crown of my head into space. Everything broke into vast light, like the sun in the sky, amazing and superb! Utterly lucid. To this day it is completely ineffable. Since there is no way to describe it, let's just say the 8th ox-herding picture… not a trace of ego-consciousness or time or particulars, just self-knowing awareness and expansive light.

Murray: Light. That's often reported in mystical experience, also in near death experiences (NDEs).

Diane: There is no conceptual framework in that state; all our words create duality.

Murray: Grammar forces us to use subject and object. Maybe music or art is a better form of expression than language.

Diane: Anyway, that wasn't psychedelics! It's important to make the distinction.

Murray: No, that was very hard work. 10 hours a day.

Diane: With feeling, not by rote.

Murray: Then what?

Diane: The following night I had a dream. There was a round pool of clean deep water. I took off all my clothes and immersed myself in it. When I came out, my old clothes had disappeared and in their place was a set of new clothes, all white. I put the new clothes on. End of dream. When I told my Tibetan Teacher about the first experience, followed by the dream the following night, he said that my actions had been purified. Goal accomplished!

Murray: In Christian terms, that dream is a second birth. You may not remember from your Christian days in Sunday School that scene when Jesus has a conversation with Nicodemus and tells him: "You must be born again." Not of the flesh but of the spirit, he added. Nicodemus went away puzzled. He couldn't fathom the mystery of a second birth. But you experienced it, and in a dream! So, this brings us to the role of dreams in liberation and individuation. You died to the old, were reborn in the new, and you put on new clothes. And what was your age at that point?

Diane: Around 33.

Murray: Not quite mid-life. Did you notice anything at mid-life?

Diane: In my early 40s we (my husband and I) went far into the Himalayas in Eastern Bhutan. The paved road ended before our destination, so the last two days we rode mountain ponies. Villagers came out to see us. Westerners were rare and they were curious. There was no running water and villagers cooked over fires. We were heading to a remote retreat centre of a famous Bhutanese Khenpo (teacher/yogi/scholar). Knowing we were coming, Khenpo had his monks prepare a type of drink to honour our visit. It was made of seven grains fermented for several days, along with other substances, and boy was it strong! We stayed at the retreat centre for about a week, and on a few occasions the teacher gave us a cup of this drink. Our translator was a Bhutanese government official who seemed thrilled to be part of this intense drinking / testing ritual. Sitting in a small hut high in the mountains, we sipped this hot drink. Once you drank it you were in a lucid, expansive state. The teacher asked questions to test our understanding of the Dharma practices we had done. Extraordinary, really. In answering, you simply couldn't be intellectual and theorize, try to please or impress the Khenpo. The drink was like a truth serum. The answer seemed to come from deep within without filters, despite what you may have wished to say. Do you think that a deep relationship with an analyst evokes similar truthful communication—just draws it from the depths?

Murray: Arriving at truth-telling is critical for analysis and individuation. It means the shadow has been cut through, also the anima is not distracting with illusions or the animus with opinions and half-baked intellectual constructions. The self can shine through and speak.

Diane: Do you think that synchronicities are also necessary for individuation? It seems to me that they are.

Murray: Are you thinking of something in particular?

Diane: I have read some of your incredible experiences of synchronicity and I know there are currently studies continuing the work of Jung and Pauli on the subject.

Murray: Have you had a strong experience of synchronicity that was transformative?

Diane: In my mid-40s I was exhausted, dark night of the soul, doubted what previously I took as self-evident. There was crisis in my working and spiritual life. I went to Marin County to stay with a friend and take a month-long course to further my career. During that month I did a day of Holotropic Breathwork with Stan Grof. Have you heard of it? It was the first time I tried it.

Murray: I do know that experience. Stan Grof came to Chicago and I attended one of his sessions. I had quite a powerful vision while breathing and listening to the music he was playing.

Diane: Well then, you know that equally important to the three hours of special breathing is the music. It starts as primitive with low, strong rhythms, then goes into an emotional section and ends with music that is peaceful and transcendent. The music together with the breathing brings you on a journey. You have one person sitting next to you as a "guardian" just holding the space, not doing the practice. You may or may not know this person— but you will be his guardian when you change places, so there is trust. When I arrived at this course in California, I had been doing a Tibetan deity meditation practice for many years. Do you know what I mean? Meditation on an archetypal deity.

Murray: Similar to active imagination, I believe. Jung did a comparative study in the 1930's and made some distinctions. But go ahead.

Diane: And on that Holotropic Breathwork session I actually *saw* the deity. I didn't lose my own identity, my own conscious stance, but was able to dialogue, ask questions, while dancing to the music. It was like being awake in a dream. I was able to communicate, express concerns, and receive feedback. And throughout the vision never faded.

Murray: That's active imagination!

Diane: That's interesting, Murray. I would like to discuss the comparisons further.

Murray: But for now, please finish the story.

Diane: That night I was energized and moved by the experience. But by the next morning I had doubts and felt silly for falling for such a fantasy. "It was illusory, made up!" I was berating myself along these lines, when I walked into a Xerox shop to copy some material on my way to the course. It was early in the morning; the shop had just opened. I was there only a few minutes, when a lady shuffled in. It looked like she had on bedroom slippers and her hair was all over the place. She presented quite an incongruent look for this part of Marin County, and I can remember her vividly to this day. I'd finished making my copies and was about to pay the store attendant, when the lady put a piece of paper on the counter in front of me, as though waiting to have it copied. I glanced at the paper and then looked again! The only thing on it was the mantra, the heart name, of the meditation deity I had seen in Holotropic Breathwork the previous day—written both in English and Tibetan script. It's one of those mind-stopping moments, I suppose like when you saw the butterfly in the Vatican.[2] You just go… blank for a few seconds.

Murray: Yes, they leave you breathless. That's exactly what I felt when I saw the butterfly dancing and then again at St. Peters in Rome.

Diane: I remember saying something to her like, "I know that mantra" and she muttered something like, "Mmmm hmmmm," picked up the paper and shuffled back out of the Xerox store. Apparently, she hadn't come in to make a copy!

Murray: An angel! She confirmed your experience with the deity.

Diane: Yes, but you don't think that way in the moment, do you? You are just stunned. Years later I described the experience to a Tibetan Lama in Nepal, and he seemed to think it was all very natural. "She was a dakini." It was

---

[2] See M. Stein, "Not Just a Butterfly."

like he was saying, "But of course, it happens all the time. Is that the first you've encountered?" (laughter)

Murray: Of course. He knew her! You seem to have entered the Tibetan celestial realm.

Diane: There and then I realized the deity is within, the archetype is within.

Murray: Within and without is interesting, isn't it? I think *within-and-without* is the watchword. Your experience shows both sides of a unitary reality. You find it within and you find it out there. Within-and-without come together in synchronicity. She is a real person. It's like the butterfly. It's a real butterfly, but it's more than a butterfly. It's a message. It's a symbol.

Diane: Murray, can you explain what you mean when you say, "both sides of a unitary reality"? Your dramatic butterfly synchronicity, which you describe in a few of your books, was not a direct result of active imagination, was it? I would like to hear more about synchronicity. Do you think it is going on all the time, but only seldom seen?

Murray: My experience of the butterfly as symbol was not in active imagination. Not at all. It was in broad daylight and while wide awake. I've had several similar synchronistic experiences around death. It seems an archetype is constellated around death, and then inner and outer seems to come together in certain objects, like the butterfly. Death creates an exceptionally fertile field for the constellation of an archetype and consequently for synchronicity. But synchronicity is a more common human experience than we might realize. Jung references using the I Ching as synchronistic, for example. A subject has a problem or question (subjective), throws the coins or yarrow stalks (objective), gets a hexagram and reads it and finds surprising correlations with the question. How does this work? By synchronicity, as Jung explains. It's strictly by chance (tossing the coins) that a match is produced. And the advice given often has surprisingly significant results if taken to heart and acted upon. What is the source of synchronicity? A hidden hand in the background, or above the head, guiding the historical event toward an end. Often one does not see the meaning of a synchronicity until later, in retrospect. The important thing about synchronicities is that they deliver meaning, and often it takes a while to let the meaning be revealed fully. The meaning is disclosed in the course of the individuation process.

Diane: Some synchronicities are very dramatic and others subtle and quiet. That evening I told my friend what happened in the Xerox shop. She had lived in Marin her whole life and said it was quite unusual to meet the woman I described. Corte Madera is a wealthy white place, and this person was neither wealthy nor white. On top of that, to have a piece of paper with the mantra in both Tibetan and English script, just that and nothing else on the paper, placing it on the counter right in front of me when the shop had just opened? I couldn't make up something like that.

Murray: (Laughter) And you just had that experience of dancing with the deity the day before.

Diane: I walked into the Xerox shop still thinking about the experience and deriding myself: "It wasn't real. I made it all up. What a fantasist I am. Get real!"

Murray: This was a message that it was real. Psyche is real! Who is that figure? Are you still working with the same figure?

Diane: Yes. I have been much of my life.

Murray: Do you use a mantra?

Diane: Not anymore, but for many years I did, yes.

Murray: Over and over and over…

Diane: Well, it's not exactly over and over and over… It's different and fresh, like a most excellent river. Is the river always the same? It's a relationship that is evolving. The practice took me through paths and stages like an inner guide, then started appearing as the Teacher in dreams, and then as synchronicities.

Murray: Is that the Teacher in the dream of the eternal flame?[3]

Diane: Yes.

Murray: Is it specifically a Tibetan deity, or is it an Indian deity?

Diane: It's both and neither. It arose quite by chance before I ever became a Buddhist. I guess it's similar to active imagination. Over the years the deity transformed from a god-like parental figure with definite characteristics, to a spiritual animus figure that I was in love with, to an inner friend, to a Wisdom Being and Teacher—sometimes simply an intuition or voice. Does that make sense?

Murray: It does to me. When you went into Jungian analysis… what were you looking for? After all these very impressive experiences of transcendence.

---

[3] See M. Stein, "The Mystery of Transcendence: A Dream for Our Time."

Diane: I couldn't square the circle. I couldn't integrate or make a bridge between the East and West, the sacred and mundane, light and dark. I felt really split by the time I began analysis. I remember crying out, "I just can't live in this divided state any longer." I felt I had reached the end of the road.

Breaking Out

Murray: I see. So, was it a moment of despair, would you say?

Diane: Yes. It was a feeling of having to break out of habits and patterns; to find a new way forward. This was reflected in my dreams as well. I kept coming to the end of the path and couldn't continue because of some wide river or steep ravine.

Murray: Is this a problem that develops among many people who take this path?

Diane: I think it's an inevitable problem that develops if you are a Westerner and go far enough with Eastern practice. If the spiritual path is more on a social or persona level, then I don't think the person would suffer much from a split. And it's probably easier to integrate Zen in the West than Tibetan Buddhism. I did a lot of Zen training, but I had a deep relationship with a Tibetan teacher in the East.

Murray: I think of the 10th picture in the Ox-herding where we see the Sage coming back into the marketplace.[4] Is that what you are looking for? Bringing them together? The marketplace is the mundane everyday world. What does Jungian analysis contribute to this process?

Diane: I didn't realize it consciously, but that was exactly what I was looking for. And what does Jungian analysis contribute? Jungian analysis, in my experience, has a huge amount to contribute. But sadly, I can't share this with many of my old friends. As soon as they hear the word "psychology" they turn off. Analysis, depth psychology, is seen as a distraction at best and evidence of a character flaw at worst! (laughter)

---

[4] See M. Stein, "Psychological Individuation and Enlightenment."

Murray: In your experience, what did Jungian analysis contribute?

Diane: I don't feel divided anymore, and that is huge. I don't feel the split between the mundane and the sacred. I sometimes realize the archetypal basis for my projections. And Jungian analysis has opened up creativity as well as meaningful relationships with all kinds of people. So Jungian analysis contributed both an understanding of my projections, and healing a painful divide.

Murray: And how does it do that?

Diane: Well, in my particular case I experienced the analyst as being a bit tough on me.

Murray: Yes?

Diane: I mean it in a good way. Before Jungian analysis I had a vague idea that psychotherapy was like sitting in front of a man who could see to the back of your skull, and then shrink you. (Laughter, both) That's exaggerating a bit, but it's a common misperception. However, Jungian analysis was completely the opposite. The analyst encouraged my own symbols and material to emerge from my psyche and we studied the material together. At first, I wasn't interested in exploring the "cellar" shadow material, even when it came up in dreams. I felt I had already done that work in my spiritual practice.

Me: "I met the shadow many times during solitary retreats."

Analyst: "And what did you do about it?"

Me: "I let it be."

Analyst: "That's not enough." And so began a fruitful relationship! He also nailed it that I'm a woman and a Westerner—not an Easterner in a feudal patriarchy. I have my own ancestral lineage and culture. He did this using my own dream material and active imagination. We worked on giving psyche equal energy to spirit, and energizing the "horizontal" dimension to balance my deeply familiar "vertical dimension."

Murray: What else did you get from your analysis?

Diane: Analysis re-awakened creativity. The analyst I worked with was also an artist so that helped. Even though I had been to art school, I suppressed that side of my personality. So, I started bringing a painting to the session every week. It was so freeing to draw inner experiences, dreams, characters. At first, I tried to depict everything in a very literal way, but gradually the paintings became freer with more feeling. Artistic expression was a big part of the individuation process for me.

Murray: Yes, I understand how important that was for you. This connection to the West is interesting. You know Jung makes a big point of staying within one's birth culture. He says it's a mistake for people from the West to go to the East and do all the work and become disconnected from their Western roots. He is very cautious about that, and he emphasizes the importance of connecting to your own ancestral history starting with your parents and then your personal ancestors.

Diane: Looking back, it was inevitable that I travelled and studied in the East. I had deep connections with a few special teachers and these connections have stayed with me even though they have long since passed away. It is invaluable to have met and studied with them, life changing. But then equally, I had to come back into my own genetics, ancestry and culture in the West. I am eternally grateful to Jung and depth psychology. It has been vital in grounding transcendent experiences into everyday life.

Murray: Great, Diane. I think it has been a wonderful conversation. It really expresses a process beautifully on an experiential level. We are not just talking about it, but really showing specifics and experience. It's very grounded. Beautiful.

CONVERSATION TWO

The Problem of Integration

Murray: Following our previous conversation, and just by chance, I was discussing Jung's book, *Aion,* with a group of students. Jung is speaking in the book about the Age of Pisces ("the Fishes"). It's a reflection on the West's religious and cultural history over the course of the last 2,000 years, thus the Age of Christianity. As you know, the fish was a symbol of Christ for the early Christians. I was reading the chapter, "The Fish in Alchemy," and came upon an account of a dream by a woman that reminded me of your description of your first LSD experience. The basic question I have now concerns the integration of experiences like yours. Experiences of the transcendent, whether you think of them as exposures to a metaphysical reality or as an opening to the unconscious, call for some type of integration with normal waking consciousness. They are a break-through to something that you hadn't seen before; the invisible becomes visible. What do you do with it? How do you work with it? Does it matter? Is it just an episodic experience that you remember occasionally, or does it have more existential significance for your life? How old were you when you had the LSD experience, by the way?

Diane: I was 19.

Murray: The dreams Jung discusses in *Aion* were also those of a young woman. Her age is not given, and I've not been able to discover who she was. My hunch is that it was Marie-Louise von Franz. I've checked with a couple of people who I thought would know, but so far it remains an open question. This young woman had a dream about a fish, and then when she came into analysis, she had another dream of a fish. The first dream was that she was standing on the bank of the Limmat River, which runs through Zurich, and looking down into the water.

> *A man threw a gold coin into the river, the water became transparent and I could see the bottom. There was a coral reef and a lot of fishes. One of them had a shining silver belly and a golden back.*[5]

That's her first dream. It's an apparently simple dream, but clearly symbolic. Then she goes into treatment, and she has the following dream.

> *I came to the bank of a broad, flowing river. I couldn't see much at first, only water, earth, and rock. I threw the pages with my notes on them into the water, with the feeling that I was giving something back to the river. Immediately afterwards I had a fishing rod in my hand. I sat*

---

[5] C.G. Jung, *Aion*, para. 236.

down on a rock and started fishing. Still I saw nothing but water, earth, and rock. Suddenly a big fish bit. He had a silver belly and a golden back.[6].

It seems to be the same fish as she saw before.

As I drew him to land, the whole landscape became alive. the rock emerged like the primeval foundation of the earth, grass and flowers sprang up, and the bushes expanded into a great forest. A gust of wind blew and set everything in motion. Then, suddenly, this whole scene becomes transformed, very alive: the rock emerged like the primeval foundation of the earth, grass and flowers sprang up, and the bushes expanded into a great forest. Then, suddenly, I heard behind me the voice of Mr. X. He said, quietly but distinctly:

"The patient ones in the innermost realm are given the fish, the food of the deep." At this moment a circle ran round me, part of it touching the water. Then I heard the voice again: "The brave ones in the second realm may be given victory, for there the battle is fought." Immediately another circle ran round me, this time touching the other bank. At the same time I saw into the distance and a colourful landscape was revealed. The sun rose over the

---

[6] Ibid.

horizon I heard the voice, speaking as if out of the distance: "The third and the fourth realms come, similarly enlarged, out of the other two. But the fourth realm"—and here the voice paused for a moment, as if deliberating—"the fourth realm joins on to the first. It is the highest and the lowest at once, for the highest and the lowest come together. They are at bottom one." Here the dreamer awoke with a roaring in her ears.[7]

Murray: Quite a dream! What did you think?

Diane: I'm thinking that Miss von Franz is asking Jung, "Do you need a close assistant for the rest of your life?!"

Murray: (Laughing) And of course that's what she did. She really formed her whole life around her relationship with Jung. Her entire life was utterly devoted to him and to his work. It became her work too, and her life merged with his interests and needs. He included her work with his own. He was generous with his recognition of her invaluable gifts. When he published *Aion* and *Mysterium Coniunctionis,* she contributed works as part of them. In the first it was an analysis of *The Passion of Perpetua*, the diary of an early Christian martyr, and in the second it was a scholarly interpretation of the medieval alchemical text, *Aurora Consurgens*. I'm thinking, these dreams of the fish in *Aion* must be of the young Marie-Louise von Franz, but I have no confirmation.

---

[7] Ibid.

Diane: The identity of the dreamer is masked, isn't it? We don't know.

Murray: No, we don't. It remains a mystery. But we do know that Miss von Franz was by his side in those years and could very likely have offered him these dreams of the fish.

Diane: Well, in the East you would say von Franz was quite ripe, as if there were lifetimes where this wisdom was ripening. It's similar to a young person who can play the piano like a genius at a ridiculously young age. She came into this life and had the potential; it was just ready to be tapped.

Murray: How do you relate to that in your experience?

Diane: My entire experience was nature, from beginning to end. The same energy that was growing the blade of grass was growing me. That intention or energy behind everything, underneath everything—alive and radiant. Not just alive as we normally think of it, but alive with meaning.

Murray: You use the word "meaning." What do you mean by "meaning"?

Diane: I wouldn't have used the word at the time—I can use it now looking back. Then, it was more like everything was imbued with... not purpose, that is too linear... energy, presence, knowledge without concept.

Murray: So, it's not intellectual, at least not yet. It's pure experience before the digestive process of reflection sets in. In the young woman's second dream as recorded in *Aion*, there are four rings, which surround her in an increasingly large diameter. That seems to have to do with integration. You could say the fish that she sees and catches is a symbol of the Self. She catches the Self in this experience, hauls this fish up, and then the voice appears and says, "The patient ones in the innermost realm are given the fish, the food of the deep." When Jung comments on this in the next paragraph, we know that the fish is miraculous food, the eucharistic food of the Eloi, the Chosen Ones. The first circle touches the water and illustrates the partial integration of the unconscious. Eating the fish is a symbol of further integration. You take it into yourself. You make it part of you. It's a eucharistic ritual. In the Catholic ritual of the Mass, you take the body and blood of Christ into yourself, and it transforms you. So, did you have the experience of integrating your breakthrough with LSD?

Diane: In the middle of the LSD experience to which you are referring, there wasn't anything to be integrated because I wasn't apart from anything. It's an experience of assimilation, you could say. You are on a substance. The question might be what was integrated later, after the LSD experience?

Murray: Yes, I see. Of course. You take something into yourself that transforms your consciousness for a period of time. Then what?

Diane: At first, on LSD for instance, the veil is lifted. I relate to that first circle. "The patient ones in the innermost realm are given the fish, the food of the deep." This to me is a glimpse of the Self, something from the unconscious that is deeply nourishing.

Murray: Yes. Digestion comes later.

Diane: And the second circle is: "The brave ones in the second realm may be given victory, for there the battle is fought." It seems the second circle is a tough integration process because that is where the battle is won. After your prolonged numinous experience, you come back down into the world of light and shadow. All kinds of habitual patterns and thoughts return.

Murray: Yes. This would be an initial phase in the process, and it might be difficult.

Diane: Back into duality. So that seems to be the battle. Going back into your ordinary ego-consciousness and into your everyday life. Tough going. You may have changed momentarily, but you will lose those insights if the battle is not fought.

Murray: So, in the first circle when you take the psychedelic substance, you are one with it. There's unity. When you come down from its effect, there's duality. Now there are two worlds, the psychedelic and the usual. Then a battle ensues. How to hold the two together, and not to lose touch with one when in the other. What happens when you split them apart is that you live either here or there. While you're here you deny there, and while you're there you deny here. They are two compartments without a door between them.

Diane: That's exactly how it is, Murray. That's the battle and that's where the victory can be won. This dream has it all in one container where everything happens. It's like a map of the whole picture. Individuation doesn't seem to be so neat and bundled.

Murray: For sure!

Diane: The battle of reconciling those two worlds takes a long time, in my experience. Others may understand it all at once, but I certainly didn't.

Murray: As you say, it's a program that you will have to live in time. You see it all suddenly. It's all there. But then you enter back into the temporal world. Individuation takes place in time, in stages, in battles won and lost. It's a complex, mixed, often confusing process. Jung doesn't say anything about the third circle, and that really puzzled me. The fourth is what brings it all together. Maybe that would be at the end of life when you have a vision that ties the whole thing together and you see the meaning of the whole. But the third...? Jung comments on the first, second and fourth, but not the third.

Diane: It's just overlooked.

Murray: Yes. Why? You know the third in Christian theology is very important. The Holy Spirit, according to theologians like St Augustine, is the love that exists between the Father and the Son. The Father first, and out of the Father comes the Son. The bond between them is the third, the Holy Spirit, who represents Love.

Diane: Could you re-word that psychologically, please? I don't relate much to this patriarchal vision of Father and Son. (Laughter) How about the love from the Self for the struggling ego-consciousness that is young and vulnerable?

Murray: OK, but it's a question of what holds the two sides together. When you go from the one to the two you have duality. What keeps them from splitting apart and becoming enemies? This happens to people. The ordinary world becomes the enemy of the transcendent world. They don't want to have anything to do with it. Vice versa, you have people who get a glimpse of the transcendent and want nothing to do with it. It's all seen as nonsense!

Diane: That is an important point, and there is evidence of it everywhere.

Murray: The third ring in the dream represents a bonding of the two. And for you, what holds the opposites together?

Diane: In the LSD experience, it was a surge of love for nature within and without. This binding together felt complete *within* the LSD experience. But then coming down can be a bit rough, to say the least. It takes a while to settle. From there on, it's a developmental process and, in my experience, a tremendous amount of work to integrate it, sometimes without success. But you have to bring the energy down and ground it, or you remain "spaced out," "burned out" or worse.

Murray: You used meditation, study, you read a lot of books, you consulted with a lot of teachers. You did a tremendous amount of meditation. Does that hold the two worlds together?

Diane: Yes. Desire for direct knowledge also holds the two together. I think many young people are idealistic and hungry for direct experience, knowledge beyond the apparent and collective, and will go to almost any length to acquire it. Many people in my generation that experimented with LSD went on to have creative careers or follow a spiritual path. The psychedelic experience was their trigger, and they then integrated it in various ways. Of course, those were the successful ones. Some never made it. We all knew people who fell under it, never able to handle the integration process or what was uncovered on the trip. It's a mistake to romanticize psychedelics—there can be disastrous results as well.

Murray: Yes, that is certainly true. I have had experience of this in my practice. Caution is needed. And what was your experience relating to meditation teachers in the East?

Diane: As you well know, there is a big difference between religious teachers who carry the letter of the doctrine, perhaps even have a grand title, but do not have wisdom. I was single-pointedly intent on finding people with whom I could dialogue, ask questions, describe experiences and get feedback. I referred to them as "wisdom beings." This was a primary concern in the first half of my life.

Murray: And did those "wisdom beings" represent somehow this visionary world? This other world, the transcendent world?

Diane: The genuine ones represented wholeness, equally transcendent and down to earth. They were imbued with humour and warmth as well as being great scholars and adepts. A joy to be around. I also met a few extraordinary yogis. But of course, by no means everyone was like that—maybe 10%. There is usually one teacher with whom you have a strong inner bond, a heart connection that feels like a destined relationship. There is an inexplicable link. In that instance, there is love, acceptance and recognition from both sides. I think it could be similar to a good analysis, where there is trust, transference, something is conveyed on a deep level. Looking back, the relationship between teacher and student was far more pivotal and enduring than any LSD trip.

Murray: That's a key point! Maybe too much emphasis is placed on the direct experience of transcendence and not enough on the relationship between student and teacher. Of course, it can tip the other way as well, with too much value placed on the guru and not enough on having a direct experience apart from that relationship.

Diane: My main connection with a "wisdom being" lasted about five years because he was very old when I met him, very old and ripened indeed. But the connection, though it takes place in time, feels eternal.

Murray: That would be the third ring in the dream.

Diane: Yes, I believe you are right. The third ring is the timeless connection with teacher or analyst. And the fourth ring, putting it into your life, living it. I'm just hesitatingly putting my baby toe into the fourth ring. (Laughter, both). I mean… seriously! The pull of the transcendent was so great it required me to go into analysis!

Murray: Yes, it's a mighty daimon.

Diane: The division is hard between the emphasis of transcendence and introversion in Eastern traditions and the bias towards extraversion and materialism in the West. After decades, the dislocation of those two opposites was so great that it "brought me to Zurich on my knees" as

43

the saying goes. To come to that point wasn't easy. So much had to be seen, admitted, and worn out.

Murray: That's what happens to some people. They get so taken with this other world that maybe began with some sort of visionary experience, but then they go to the East and they don't come back. Or they have a very hard time coming back. It becomes a geographical split between the East and the West. Coming back to the West is a downer.

Diane: I know people who have not come back, and it hasn't worked out for them. Often, they get to a stage in life where they are too old to make the transition back. It's easy to sympathize with them, though. In the West, you get the impression that inner work, the psyche or spirit, isn't valued. Generally speaking, you can't find that support. For instance, how many hermits are respected and honoured in the West? The East loves their hermit-saints. I suppose Brother Klaus of Switzerland was the last generation of that tradition. You just can't have that dialogue in the West. People think you are morbid. (Laughter). Also, much of the general public regards Eastern spiritual centers in the West with suspicion. They are seen as cultish.

Murray: In Jungian circles, the figure of Robert Johnson comes to mind. He loved the East and spent a good deal of time there. Coming back was a real stress for him. And religion can certainly be a cause for division and shadow projection.

Diane: Yes, institutionalized religion can be a problem in relationships and also a barrier to mystical experience.

You can get lost for years, decades, following a religious creed or dogma. Life's questions have all been answered and codified for you; you are encouraged to put up and shut up. (Laughter) About 15 years ago, in a private meeting with the Dalai Lama about climate change in the Himalayas, he ended our interesting discussion with the friendly advice to *take off your Buddhist hat*. What a gift—the universal life, the symbolic life.

Murray: What you say takes me to another passage a little later in *Aion* that I want to look at with you. I'm going to start with a passage that Jung quotes from an alchemist:

"This stone is below thee as to obedience; above thee as to dominion; therefore from thee, as to knowledge; about thee, as to equals." The passage is somewhat obscure. Nevertheless, it can be elicited that the stone stands in an undoubted psychic relationship to man: the adept can expect obedience from it, but on the other hand the stone exercises dominion over him. Since the stone is a matter of "knowledge" or science, it springs from man. But it is outside him, in his surroundings, among his "equals," i.e., those of like mind.[8]

Now this is the passage I wanted to look at closely.

This description fits the paradoxical situation of the self, as its symbolism shows. It is the

---

[8] Ibid., para. 257.

smallest of the small, easily overlooked and pushed aside. Indeed, it is in need of help and must be perceived, protected, and as it were built up by the conscious mind, just as if it did not exist at all and were called into being only through man's care and devotion. As against this, we know from experience that it had long been there and is older than the ego, and that it is actually the secret *spiritus rector* of our fate.[9]

Diane: That's certainly well said, isn't it?

Murray: Isn't that strong? Jung at his best. The self does not become conscious by itself, but has always been taught by traditions of knowing, of Gnosis. This is what you came to in Tibetan Buddhism, a tradition of knowing.

> Since it stands for the essence of individuation, and individuation is impossible without a relationship to one's environment, it is found among those of like mind with whom individual relations can be established.[10]

Diane: Ah….so beautiful!

Murray: Jung does mention on occasion that you can't individuate outside of relationship. But this is a very strong statement about the value of traditions and communities. Our conversations are about liberation, about liberating the Self from its closed, hidden condition

---

[9] Ibid.
[10] Ibid.

in the unconscious. Traditions can help people liberate the Self from unconsciousness. We need the support of people of like mind. I think you found that in various communities. You probably don't need it now because it's well planted in you. But at least for a period of time that connection with a Guru or a Sangha was necessary.

Diane: You are correct. In my experience it is essential, like growing a seedling inside a greenhouse until it's ready to be planted outdoors. It is incredibly beneficial and necessary, as Jung says. But if continued too long perhaps it can turn into its opposite. It's a strong statement from Jung. The relationship between Teacher and student has been abused in the West, but when it's authentic, the relationship is pivotal.

Murray: This is also the rationale for analysis. It takes two persons in the room and a deep relationship between them.

Diane: It's true for all human endeavours, isn't it? A young talented musician having a relationship with a great music teacher will make all the difference. It will bring out the student's potential. I think it's vital, non-negotiable, to have a one-to-one relationship with a genuine teacher, whatever the field.

Murray: So, liberation is not a solitary endeavour, and the same holds true for individuation.

Diane: In the spiritual world, it means having a teacher who is a real holder of an authentic wisdom lineage. Not easy, but sometimes it drops into your lap.

Murray: There is a notion of "transmission" in the East. I don't think we have that in the West. In the bond that forms between the teacher and the student, or guru and disciple, something gets passed on in a very subtle way. It isn't just through verbal teaching.

Diane: As is said in Zen, and this is true in Dzogchen as well, the real transmission is outside the scriptures. When I was around 37, my main teacher told me "our minds have already mixed."

Murray: Jung writes about this in his essay on transference.

Diane: It must be similar. The teacher, or analyst, can sense when the time is ripe. My teacher was telling me that even if we weren't able to meet in person anymore, the transmission would continue to develop within me if I continued the work. He passed away soon after that.

Murray: You know, in analysis there are levels of relationship and communication. At the upper level, it's people talking to each other, and at the deeper level there is a transmission or a union of energies.

Diane: That union of energies opens doors, doesn't it? If you have a strong *intent* toward knowledge, Gnosis, and you keep it pure and singular, the right situations will find you even if you don't go searching for them. No doubt. If you are determined, you will be led.

Murray: That's trust in synchronicity. Don't the Chinese say that when the student is ready, the teacher will appear? If you are engaged seriously in intent, and touch upon the archetypal level, something constellates and then doors start opening.

Diane: Something constellates and doors open. That's a great way of describing it.

Murray: Now I would like to shift to your dream of the eternal fire on the 5th floor, which comes in your 60s.[11] The dream is of discovering something that has probably always been there. It's a breakthrough dream. You come up the stairs, discover another level, and open the door. Inside the room you see this fire. At first you don't know what it is. You are concerned that it might destroy the building, until you realized that it's not burning up anything. It's self-sustaining. It's an eternal fire. You realize the Self is in you, in your house. It's right there. It has always been there, and now you are coming into its presence. So that is something to metabolize, digest, integrate. You realize that it's part of your house, the god within. It's divine. The eternal fire is a god image. It's eternal, like God is eternal. But it's within your house.

The Eternal Fire

[11] M. Stein, "The Mystery of Transcendence - A Dream for Our Time," in *The Mystery of Transformation*, Chiron Publications, 2022.

Diane: Without going anywhere, you arrive at your destination.

Murray: Yes, within your own psyche. Jung talks about integration a bit later in the text. About half-way through he speaks about fixation. Fixation is an alchemical term; it fixes something or holds it in place. Jung emphasizes the importance of "concepts" for this operation of fixation: "For without the existence of conscious concepts apperception is, as we know, impossible."[12] This is what traditions give you. They give names for these images we experience in dreams and visions. And this is also what Jungian psychology gives us. "Oh, it's the Self!" we may say of a dream like yours. You have to have these concepts in order to fix it. Without these tools, the contents revealed sink back into the unconscious and create psychological problems:

> This explains numerous neurotic distur-bances which arise from the fact that certain contents are constellated in the unconscious but cannot be assimilated owing to the lack of apperceptive concepts that would 'grasp' them. This is why it is so extremely important to tell children fairy-tales and legends, and to inculcate religious ideas (dogmas) into grown-ups, because these things are instrumental symbols with whose help unconscious contents can be canalized into consciousness, interpreted, and integrated.[13]

---

[12] Ibid., para. 259.
[13] Ibid.

Jung is putting great value here on traditional stories and teachings, again to help a person to integrate these breakthrough experiences, to fix them and hold them in consciousness with meaning. Here is the image you drew placing the fire discovered on the 5th floor, right in the middle of the house.[14]

The Inner Courtyard

This gives the numinous experience and content the centrality it needs. Otherwise, it might bring about a burning within, a neurosis, namely a split between the lower levels of the house and the uppermost level.

---

[14] See M. Stein, *The Mystery of Transformation*, pp. 6ff. for further details.

Diane: It is taking so long to integrate this dream! For instance, it took at least three years to see the fire in the center of the house and paint it as you see it above. I've produced many paintings on this dream, had many discussions, and now understand how essential it is to work with a big dream in every way you can. Sometimes I still wonder, what is that flame in the middle of the house? In Zen you might be asked, what is your face before you were born? Maybe it's this timeless fire. Murray, what does *your* face look like before you were born?

Murray: I have some hints from dreams, but I keep them secret. It's my personal myth.

Diane: Of course, you can't say! But I get a special dispensation since I'm not an analyst, right?

Murray: Well, you were told by the teacher that people would be coming to see it and to keep the door open, so it's a bit different. You have the sides of the house: one, two, three and four, don't you? And then the flame in the central circle is the quintessential, the fifth.

Diane: The eternal fire was always there before the house, and made the house possible. But the house was also essential for the discovery of the fire, or the Self.

Murray: This painting shows integration of a mystical or numinous experience.

Diane: I wonder, is there such a thing as the central fire being *liberated* from the four "walls" of the body experientially? That's what is described in the Advaita Vedanta tradition. There is also a lot of research into NDEs which speak of unbounded light, and then the person returns to the "four walls" when they re-enter the body. However, what is less expressed is what is experienced when the divine fire returns into the *house of the body.* I guess that's what Jung suffered in the hospital returning to health after his beatific visions. The brightness is covered over, dimmed almost beyond recognition. It's as if Plato steps out of the cave and sees the endless blue sky and shining sun, but then suddenly, wham, he is back in the cave looking at the shadows on the wall again. Try telling him to integrate that vision of the sky and sun while back in the dark shadow cave. How can there be integration of that?!

Murray: That's the challenge, Diane.

Diane: It's like swallowing a diamond. Digest that!

Murray: However, in your dream you have another stage suggested by the teacher. I think we might associate it with the 10th ox-herding picture. He says, "people will come—share the room." That's the next step. Once it's fixed and in place—and you have the image—what to do with it? You don't want to digest it and dissolve it. It isn't digestion in that sense. No, it's important to hold the image and to open the door. It's an invitation for... what? *A kind of extraverted utilization of the Self,* as you have found it and fixed it. How to share that space in a way that is safe?

Diane: *An extraverted utilization of the Self.* What a powerful instruction. Hold the image and open the door? I suppose we have our great artists, poets, and musicians who do that for us, open the door of the Self so, for a while, we can experience it non-verbally. But everyone has these experiences of the Self, whether recognized and integrated or not, don't they? Whether expressed creatively or not. But if one describes transcendent experiences through ego's lens it sounds inflated and pretentious.

Murray: I understand.

Diane: Opening the door doesn't have to be formal or a professional calling?

Murray: No, it can be unspoken and subtle. It can be hospitality. Think of Philemon and Baucis.

Diane: Welcome, disguised gods…Come in! Dinner is served.

Murray: Well, yes. Isn't everyone a god in disguise? Sometimes very well disguised, I have to admit. But still… What do people do with their great visions? You can become an evangelist. But I don't think you want to do that! You can become an author. You can do what we're doing here, sharing in dialogue. Maybe some kind of written statement or publication can come out of these conversations. I think there are many ways to keep that door open without injuring yourself. But you have to be careful. There are some things that you have to keep secret, that diamond within. You don't want to throw it in front of someone who has no understanding whatsoever and will…

Diane: …trash it.

Murray: Scorn and ridicule it, perhaps out of envy. That's not good for you. That's not good for anyone. So, you have to be careful. I wonder, if this was Marie-Louise von Franz's dream, why didn't she tell anybody? The people I talked with about the dream were very close to her. She gave one of them 200 of her dreams in her estate, willed to him, but that dream is not among them. So, he thinks that couldn't be her dream because she would have told him about it. I have a hunch that she kept it secret because it was so precious and so special. Jung used it in this text, and she didn't want to damage it in any way by saying "Oh, that's mine."

Diane: Also, she wouldn't want to have a lesser mortal interpret it. Only Jung. (Laughter, both)

Murray: Ok Diane, we will have to end here for today. This has been an important and interesting discussion on the importance of integrating numinous experiences.

CONVERSATION THREE

Pictures from Analysis

Diane: Murray, these are a series of pictures I painted during my three years in analysis. They are based on dreams and presented chronologically. I'm curious if the work you've done with clients over many years follows a universal course of individuation, more or less, with common themes and motifs. Needless to say, everyone is individual and each analysis unique, but maybe we can see common movement in the direction of wholeness. I would like to see if we can do this based on the pictures, without referring to specific dream content.

Murray: That could be interesting. You could tell something about the image, without dream content, and I would offer a commentary. As you said, every analysis is unique, and yet all are guided by similar archetypal patterns of development if the analysis goes at all deep. In offering a commentary, I will keep it minimal so as to allow center stage to the images. The reader and I will contemplate the images together, and this will be meant to allow them to communicate information that goes beyond verbal articulation. We want to let the images speak.

Diane: Before we start, can we discuss the difference between "art" and pictures made as part of an analysis.

Murray: Yes. That is an important distinction, especially in your case.

Diane: As I was looking at these 24 pictures yesterday, I was knocked over by how childish and naïve they are. They would be laughed out of first year art school. They couldn't be shown to my artist friends, let alone put in an art gallery or sold. They are stripped of conventional artistic standards. I find them embarrassing and compelling at the same time. Why? I think it's because they are pre-reason. Although candid and naked in their depiction of images from the unconscious, they lack artistic sophistication. There is a vulnerability, as though an 8-year-old drew them, as though one is under the spell of the dream. Even now, a decade later, as I look at the pictures I am immediately in touch with the freshness of the dream as if it was yesterday. The only thing that has changed is perhaps a maturation of my understanding of the symbol and meaning.

Murray: I'm reminded of Carl Jung playing in his back garden—some sticks, stones, water and earth would delight and clear his mind as he made castles and fortifications. Playing like this returned him to a non-rational source of creativity and fresh insights would arise in his mind. To an onlooker, it might be disturbing to see a grown man, a psychiatrist, a father of five children playing like a child in his garden during the noon-hour. Embarrassing to be seen like this? He didn't care. It's similar to painting images for analytic purposes. All the refined learning that has been so painstakingly acquired has to be put aside in order for the unconscious to have a space to speak and show itself. It's not "art" in the conventional sense of the word. The patient is not concerned with working within a tradition of painting ancient or contemporary. This is soul work, not art work.

Diane: This is why, I think, most people I know don't want to go anywhere near analysis or the unconscious. It's humiliating. It upends the sophisticated and refined way of communicating and seeing the world that has been built up since childhood.

Murray: The trained artist, like yourself, is handicapped because of all the inhibitions and constraints imposed by trends and conventions. Harold Bloom spoke of "anxiety of influence" with respect to poets. They are constantly looking over their shoulder at what their predecessors have done, either secretly quoting them or working against their influence for the sake of something "new" and "creative." Pictorial artists are the same. Are you painting like Kandinsky, or like Frank Stella? Are you aware of your predecessors and of the trends that have taken over lately? This is working within culture. It might also contribute to consciousness on a collective level. Artists have a central role to play in individuation of cultures and spirituality. But working with art materials in analysis has a different purpose. It serves the individuation process of the individual. This may mean making pictures that don't fit in with the styles and preferences of the art world as it exists in the day.

Diane: In your practice as an analyst over the last 50 years, how important is creating a visual representation of dream material or active imagination?

Murray: It's always useful. It deepens and stabilizes the inner work.

Diane: Does painting dreams invoke the spirit of the depths and take the dream to a more symbolic level?

Murray: If one allows the eye to lead, not the head, then, yes, it adds to the symbolic effect. That's because the unconscious is further engaged. Painting is a form of active imagination. As we will see, following the prompting of the spirit of the depths (in your series, picture number one, the golden salmon) takes you on a journey inward, not outward, at least for the time being.

Diane: In your own analysis did you paint your dreams or active imagination?

Murray: Yes, of course. It was implicitly required as a part of analysis. This is, after all, the Jungian program. But I didn't feel pressured or compelled. It was an addition to the work that flowed easily for me. Painting also taught me to look at things more closely.

Diane: For me, I can't imagine a successful analysis without painting images that arise. No matter how literal my attempt to capture the *actual* dream symbol, something not previously seen—from the unconscious—pops out in the drawing.

Murray: Exactly. The unconscious reveals itself in the act of painting. It's a bit uncanny, don't you think?

Diane: Very uncanny! At first it was a real struggle. I had to loosen the controlling hand of artistic training and sensibility in order to let the unconscious speak. I always had the feeling someone was looking over my shoulder, criticizing a lack of subtlety or sophistication. But when I let go there were surprising results! For instance, the expression on the face of a human or animal often captured something of which I was unaware. No explanations or descriptions on the part of myself or the analyst could bring that material out into the open like the painting did.

Murray: That means the image is alive. It leads; it's not your ego and artistic training leading.

Diane: A vulnerability and rawness comes through in drawings of dreams, at least in my experience. It's a bit edgy. It makes all the difference if it's witnessed by someone who understands the process.

Murray: That would be the role of the analyst. The analyst is there to appreciate, not to criticize. The analyst is not a painting instructor.

Diane: You will notice, Murray, in these 24 pictures the dreamer is depicted as a young lady or even a girl. This wasn't an attempt at self-glorification, it's how ego-consciousness sees itself in relation to the unconscious—young, naïve, a student. Is this common?

Murray: Absolutely. We call it regression in the service of the self. Again, we will see this process at work in the pictures you made, even to the point of death and rebirth. Actually, the psyche is ever young and ever ancient. True creativity depends on the ability to go with the flow of process, sometimes forward and sometimes backward. Jung once spoke of "doing the self." Individuation is an activity. And may we always be students and not become rigid old professors repeating their lessons year after year until they lose their voice in the grave.

Diane: That's powerful and spot on. Keeping all that in mind, let's look at the pictures together.

No. 1: The Pregnant Salmon

Diane: In the picture you see the dreamer standing on rocks on the banks of a wide river, backed by low mountains. There is no bridge. A great golden salmon, much larger than life, suddenly leaps high out of the river spraying water in every direction. The salmon seems to indicate: "Follow me!" The fish is swimming to the left and upstream to lay her eggs.

Murray: This is what is called "an initial dream" in analysis. Initial dreams are taken to be forecasts of the direction the analysis will take. The golden fish signals the dreamer to turn left, i.e., into the unconscious. Following this guidance from the Self, which is represented here as a pregnant salmon, will mean taking a turn to intense introversion and a journey to the inner source of new life and the creative center of the psyche. It means following the spirit of the depths and leaving the spirit of the times. The dream is numinous and indicates a positive message to the analysand about the future course of the analysis. Following such a dream, one will look for offspring, so-called "spawn," in future dreams and images. Initial dreams often forecast the future of the analysis. Obviously, this one is off to a good start. The fish/Self has shown itself in a marvellous leap upward into the world of consciousness. This dream is a kind of initiation into the world of the unconscious. We might also think of it as an invitation to others to follow the same path toward individuation. Even societies and cultures. Look to the depths of the collective unconscious for clues of what is to come!

No. 2: *Prima Materia*

Diane: Here is a rich gathering of content—dark, light, solid, delicate. The picture has layers and layers of depth, one on top of the other so you cannot separate them or see clearly. The white lines give it movement and a sense that something is being created. However, it is also confusing. No area is emphasized. Can anything significant emerge from this rich confusion?

Murray: This is what you find in the depths if you follow the salmon: All the necessary ingredients for a future process have been gathered and are available. All of life as lived so far is brought into the space of consciousness and made available for new forms to take shape in the cauldron of the opus. More than that, all the potentials not yet lived. Alchemists had recipes for the opus. If you get the right ingredients and apply heat under carefully constructed conditions, a process of transformation will ensue. The ingredients will cook, then there will be distillations, and finally the essence will be extracted. This is the soul hidden in matter, in the depths of the unconscious. The *prima materia* is the archetypal core of the psyche in all its aspects, conscious and unconscious. Can something valuable be extracted and distilled from this *massa confusa*? An essence, the soul, something to sustain a meaningful life in the future? This is the hope we have at the beginning of the opus.

No. 3: Darkness at the Beginning

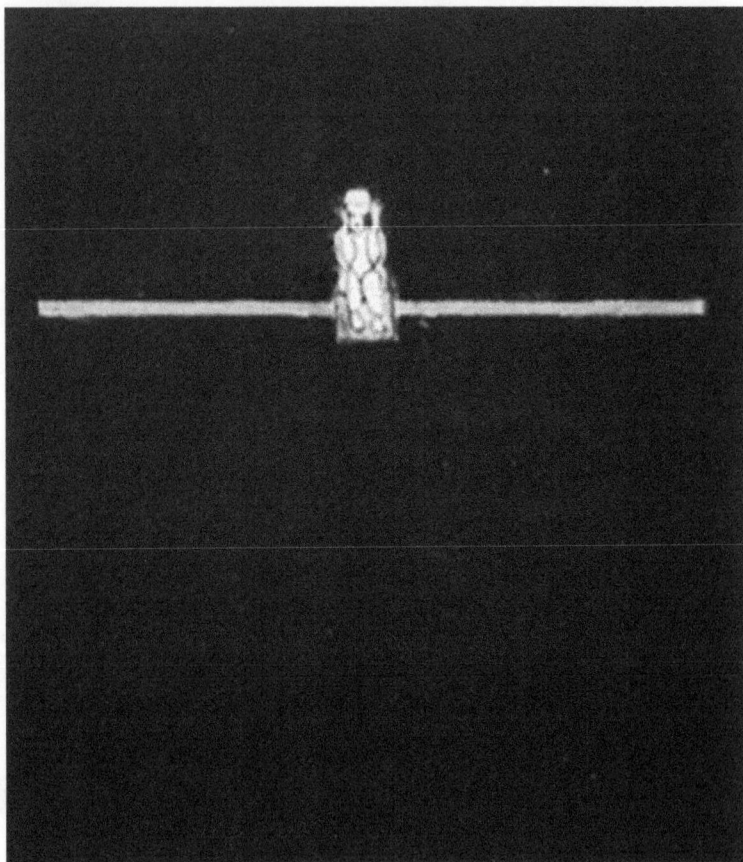

Diane: In this picture, we see a small white figure with head in hands, sitting precariously on a white ledge suspended in space. The surrounding area is completely black with no reference point. Where is the person located in space and time? Is it a nightmare? Has the dreamer lost her identity? The surrounding space is completely black; no hint of moon, star or guiding light. And yet the figure itself is white, as is the ledge. Somehow, it doesn't look hopeless.

Murray: The psychic condition at this moment is of one who is isolated, without much support, and immersed in the inner work. This is the beginning of the process. The alchemists called it "nigredo," blackness. And they said, "rejoice when this happens." It means the process has begun. What a strange way to begin a journey! But this is the nature of individuation. It's not a joyride at Disneyland with your friends. This is a moment of coming to oneself in the descent of introversion. Most people are afraid of this and fall back on their defences. They may leave analysis claiming it is not for them or with anger toward the charlatan analyst. Cultures and societies do the same. It's natural to want to feel good and be optimistic about a brilliant future. But if the defenses rule, the opus comes to a stop. The adept leaves the laboratory, and the fires go out. It's a challenge for the analyst to keep the fires burning when the patient despairs.

No. 4: Wind

Diane: This picture is quite exciting after the last one. Although there is a lot of darkness, there is no feeling of being stuck. The wind blows in every direction and goes where it will. Formations and patterns of light look like something is about to take form. The image resembles a powerful, impersonal force of nature. The dreamer's fate is in the hands of the gods.

Murray: I love this picture. It's so suggestive. I can see many figures suggested in the darkness. The spirit (*pneuma*) begins to move over the dark waters, stirring the surface and creating movement. Energy is emerging in the stillness of the unconscious. Though still in the condition of *nigredo*, there is strong, swirling movement in this picture. Light appears at the top, and bubbles of light are coming to the surface. This picture gives us the feeling of the unfathomable creative power of the unconscious. It is said that "the darkness has its own light." The opus is underway.

No. 5: Meeting the Snake

Diane: The snake in the picture is regal. She is wearing a precious jewel. Is this a Queen of Snakes? She is against both a light and black background and looks unconcerned by the presence of the observer. Although the body of the snake is in a position to strike, the expression suggests otherwise.

Murray: This is dramatic! Where did this snake come from? Obviously, it came out of the *prima materia*. What we see in this picture is a direct encounter with Mercurius, the spirit of the unconscious. What is most startling about the picture is the snake's hooded eyes. They are looking directly and steadily at the viewer. It's the opportunity for a connection between the unconscious spirit of the depths and the conscious personality of the dreamer. The eyes are fascinating, mesmerizing. It's amazing that the snake, so far removed from human consciousness, has come so near. Usually, we think of this level of the unconscious as being completely out of reach. The unconscious is reaching out to the dreamer's conscious world, willing to make contact. Of course, there is a natural fear of snakes in most people. They have a chilling effect, and it takes a while to feel comfortable with them. This is the way we tend to feel about the unconscious. Freud used the word *unheimlich* ("uncanny") to describe this effect of the unconscious upon the ego. The task in analysis is to get used to it and to befriend it. It is the "inner other," to use Jung's words.

No. 6: Division

Diane: In this picture, a circular sphere is divided. The left half of the circle is lighter and smaller than the right. The center of the mandala is bright—is it empty or full? It's hard to say. The other areas in the picture are hard, straight, definite lines. These areas enter into the circle from both sides. It looks abstract and impersonal, but has more form than the last picture.

Murray: The picture has a certain amount of harmony. The two sides are held together, but they are not communicating. In alchemy this is called *separatio*: "Only what has been separated can be united." Individuation requires both separation and union. Analysis brings consciousness to bear on the *prima materia*, and this differentiates the material that we saw in picture 2. As a consequence, the whole is organized into pairs of opposites, the greatest being the division between conscious and unconscious. On the left we see the unconscious; on the right, the conscious. In analysis, we would try to discover what is on each side of the divide running vertically through the picture. On the other hand, it is a picture of wholeness. We can see both sides contained within a mandala, which has a brilliant center. The mandala is not split to such an extent that the pieces fall apart. The snake would be on the left side of the image, and the conscious world on the right side. In analysis, one becomes aware of the opposites in oneself and between our instincts and our persona.

No. 7: Tracing the Left Hand

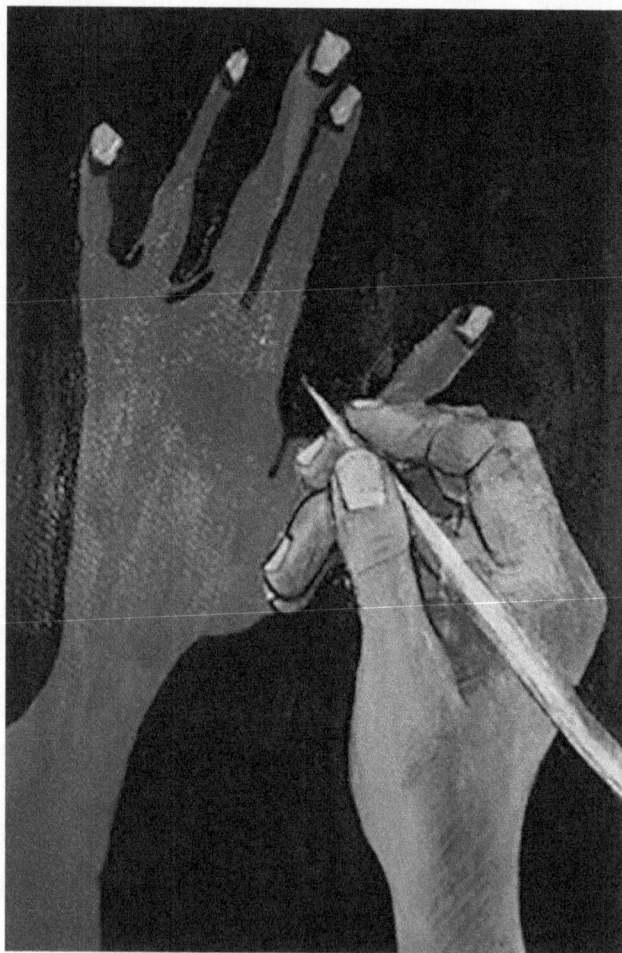

Diane: This picture shows a right hand holding a pencil with confidence. The left hand is dark and looks atrophied, as though it hasn't been used and is withering away. In comparison to the fleshy quality of the right hand, the left looks flat. Don't the fingernails on the left hand look odd? As if they are gold, metallic, or even claws.

Murray: The right hand, developed and in control of the pencil, is tracing the shape of the other side of the personality, the unconscious. The right hand is healthy and capable, a superior function. The left hand is inferior and misshapen—left behind in the dark. Tracing the contours of the left hand is a type of shadow work, discovering the contours of the inferior function(s), the undeveloped and rejected ones. This is slow and painstaking work in analysis, but so important in the second half of life. In theology, Satan is called "the left hand of God." The left hand does things that the right hand does not know about but it is also in the service of the Self. We try to make it conscious. In the end, both hands are needed to deal with the challenges of living the individuation process. This is a picture of self-examination and discovery. It's a dialogue. Would that this could take place also in the world of politics and finance.

No. 8: Meeting William-Sophia in the Woods

Diane: This is a surprise image! The dreamer comes suddenly across a two-headed child in the middle of a path in the woods. The child is delighted to see the observer. William-Sophia, as the title tells us, looks to be about 6 or 7 and is stretching out their arms to be hugged. Has the child been abandoned in the woods? There is no sign of parents in the picture, and every sign that the child would like to be accepted (and adopted) by the dreamer.

Murray: What a charming image. This is the syzygy, as Jung calls it, the young anima and animus before they become separated and form a one-sided identity. There is such innocence to this picture. It shows an early form of oneness. The syzygy shows the joy of unity of play and work, rational thinking and intuitive feeling, a marvellous transitional state of being. The dreamer has discovered the "inner child," who is not yet distorted by conventional forces that press for adaptation to cultural expectations. This child is unspoiled. This is a promising forerunner of the later *unio mentalis*, the union of soul and spirit, which will be a fruit of the individuation process. The spawn laid by the golden salmon are hatching and showing the potential for wholeness. In this picture, the feminine is in the foreground, the masculine behind and supportive. This will be the identity of this individual – love in the foreground, rational thinking supportive in the background. Notice the two right hands! On a cultural level, this would be a whole new type of culture, and I believe it is something that we sorely need in our world.

No. 9: Death of the Yogi in a Tower

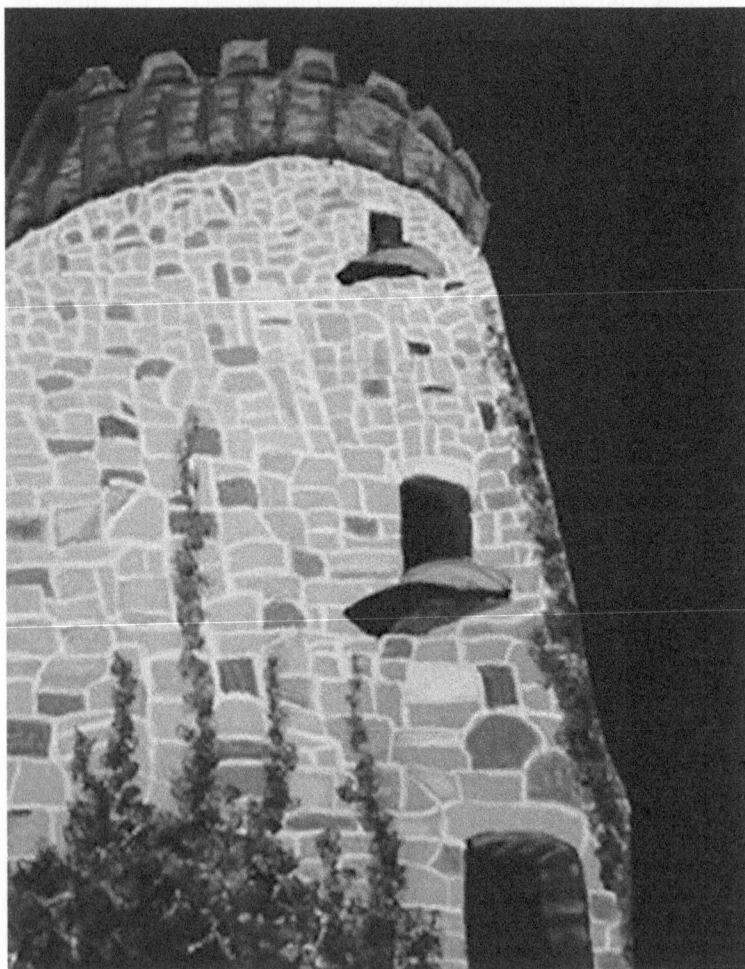

Diane: We see a tall tower made of various shades of stone. It appears to be night and yet the stones provide a glow. Ivy is growing up the tower on both sides. Although it's a well-proportioned building, it doesn't look very inviting. It seems cold and dark inside and out.

Murray: The high stone tower with a dark entrance door and two small windows in the picture indicate a strong degree of defense and interiority. It does strike the viewer as cold and forbidding. The Yogi who lived here was separated totally from the surrounding world of nature and society. It was a life of total introversion, dedicated to the spiritual life exclusively. Now this is passing away because a new stage or phase of life is emerging. Ivy is growing up the sides of the tower. Soon the tower will be covered with it. Ivy is generally considered to be a symbol of faithfulness and close attachment, even of love. I imagine that the tower will remain available for retreats by others in the future. It is a place of interiority and spirituality and not to be abandoned or to fall into disrepair. The ivy seems to be a sign of new life and protection for the tower. One wonders who the new occupants will be. I am thinking of Jung's tower at Bollingen. He didn't live there but he used it as a place of retreat. He said he felt most himself when he was there. The tower is a precious symbol of solitude.

No. 10: Child and Mother

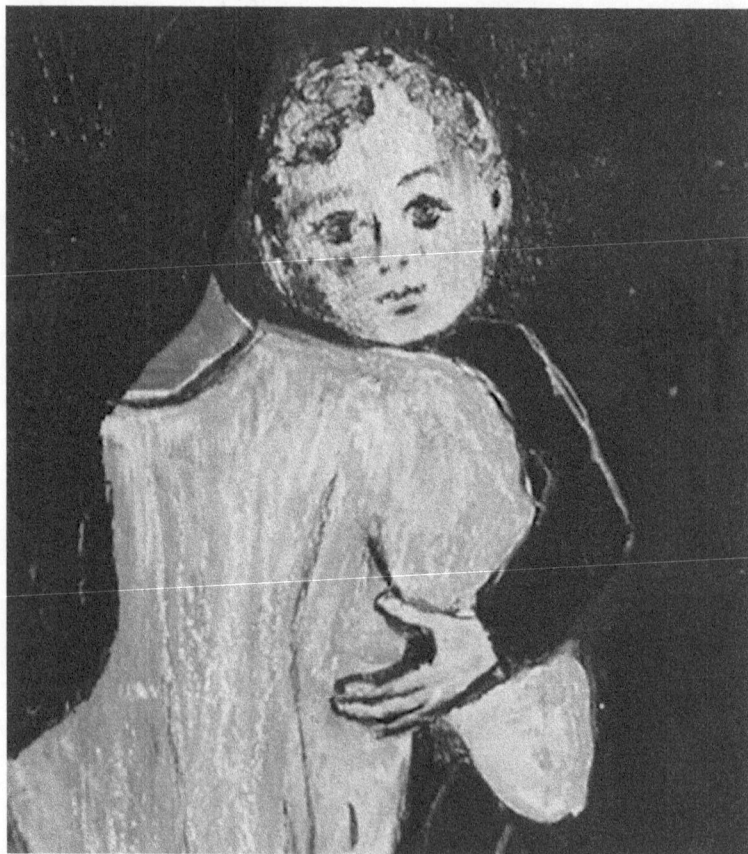

Diane: This beautiful child can't see the mother's face, but the image suggests she is holding him securely and the child is serene. His eyes are a central feature of the picture, and communicate an interest in us, the viewers.

Murray: The young child is holding lightly to its mother, the very picture of innocence. The child is without fear and is a symbol of futurity, pure potentiality. This little one has a whole life ahead of it. The wide eyes show curiosity and naivety. This is a new beginning. In the series of pictures, it follows the death of the hermit Yogi in the cold tower. There, coldness and death; here, warmth and life. What a contrast! Death followed by rebirth is an archetypal pattern. The mother's face is not seen by the child or by us, but her figure is solid and reliable. For a child, the mother is the Great Goddess and represents the whole world. This is a picture of a secure relationship, also in the analytic field since this occurs in that context. The new being is firmly held in relationship, which augurs well for the future. The child is looking directly at us with a trusting, wholesome, curious gaze, taking in everything.

No. 11: Trickster Appears

Diane: This fox character is almost impossible to control or catch. He comes and goes at will, outrageously stealing things, as well as leaving unexpected gifts. He has shifty eyes. No matter how many times and ways the dreamer tries to catch him, he is always one step ahead.

Murray: It's Mercurius, the spirit of the unconscious. A fox, the opposite of the naïve child in the previous picture, is canny. He is standing in a field, alert and with intensely focused eyes. The manifestation of this trickster figure indicates a strong constellation of the unconscious. The unconscious is a part of the personality that can't be pinned down or controlled. It has a will of its own, usually contrary to conscious identity and intentions. Its manifestation is not without its dangers. The fox can lead one into the ditch. Or, it can guide one to hidden treasures in the Self. This picture introduces liminality, the betwixt-and-between space between stable states of identity. A major change is about to get underway.

No. 12: The Meditation Box

Diane: The background of this painting is more interesting than the figure in the box! The swirls and dance of the energy are fascinating and full of life. By comparison the box looks dead and empty. But the longer I gaze at the image, the more I appreciate the contrast between the inner stillness of the meditation box and the dramatic movement outside.

Murray: Yes, stillness in a field of energetic turbulence. A figure, anonymously dressed in a dark robe, sits in a thick protective frame, a secluded space perfect for meditation and interiority. Her back is to us, unlike the preceding pictures of the child and the fox. She has turned away from the outer world. She faces a plain white wall without images to distract her mind. Outside the box, dynamic forces swirl in every direction. The "10,000 things" are kept away from her so that deep insight and strength may develop within. This picture encourages the viewer to do the same: turn inward, shut down your cell phones and Internet connections for a while, put your daily duties and responsibilities to the side, look at the blank space in the back of your mind and stay there for a while. If enough people would do this, the world would slow down a bit from its frantic pace. The planet would also enjoy the break from our ceaseless activities. The black box is a sacred space. Everyone who enters here is protected from the world outside and able to experience the god within the temple of the mind.

No. 13: Night Sea Journey

Diane: This picture is a turbulent sea at night. The black depths of the water indicate that the boat is far from land. The ship looks like a car-passenger ferry with many windows and levels. As large as it is, it's no match for the enormous waves that surround it. It's hard to predict a safe outcome for the dreamer, passengers and ferry.

Murray: The night sea journey is an archetypal passage from death (the setting of the sun) to new life (the dawn of a new day). This passage is threatened by demons and devils that arise from their caves in the Underworld. It is never certain that the journey will succeed in making its way to the new day. Prayers are sung and chanted for the safety of the storm-tossed barque. This is a dangerous and critical passage. Setting out for a new life, the dreamer is plunged into turbulence and feelings of confusion. The sun makes this journey through the underworld every night. It's a scary time. The monsters of the deep threaten the solar barque as it makes its way to a new dawn in the East. Things are unstable on the high seas. Yet, the ship looks strong enough for the journey.

No. 14: Under Water

Diane: This picture shows the dreamer's outline under water. Perhaps the dreamer has drowned in the storm. It looks like there is a target on the dreamer's heart. Is this a mandala or a burial at sea? There is considerable movement and bubbles of light in the picture. The outcome is uncertain.

Murray: The safety of the collective, the ferry boat, has vanished. It is now an individual story of making the passage to a new life. This is actually the core of the initiation process; a baptism in the dark waters of the unconscious. Although the outcome is uncertain, the picture suggests rebirth into greater consciousness by the mandala pattern of light, which is centered on the heart of the initiate. In the world of dreams, being underwater means the ego is immersed in the unconscious. This might manifest as being temporarily out of touch with material reality and floating in a sea of fantasy, a dissociated state of mind. This is not necessarily dangerous or a bad thing, provided it does not go on too long. It is part of the Night Sea Journey of individuation.

No. 15: The Queen's Gift

Diane: We see a Queen dressed in full regalia with a ceremonial staff in her right hand. This sceptre is a symbol of her power. The Queen wears a bejewelled necklace holding a precious gem. Her crown is of unusual design, with seven jewels. She is an impressive figure and although her stance is upright and authoritative, her expression is both serious and warm. The young dreamer is facing away from the sea and studying the waves as they are reflected in the mirror (the Queen's gift).

Murray: The Self appears as Queen and bestows the gift of a round mirror, which the young initiate holds in her left hand. We know the sea is at her back by the reflection of waves in the mirror. She has survived the ordeal of the Night Sea Journey and arrived on the far shore. The Queen seems to be giving instructions to observe the movements and fluctuations of the waves and tides in a reflective way, not directly. This symbolizes an objective attitude toward the inner world and protects against over-identification with archetypes and complexes. The Self is the teacher, instructing the initiate to have greater detachment and objectivity in relating to the unconscious.

No. 16: The Philosophical Tree

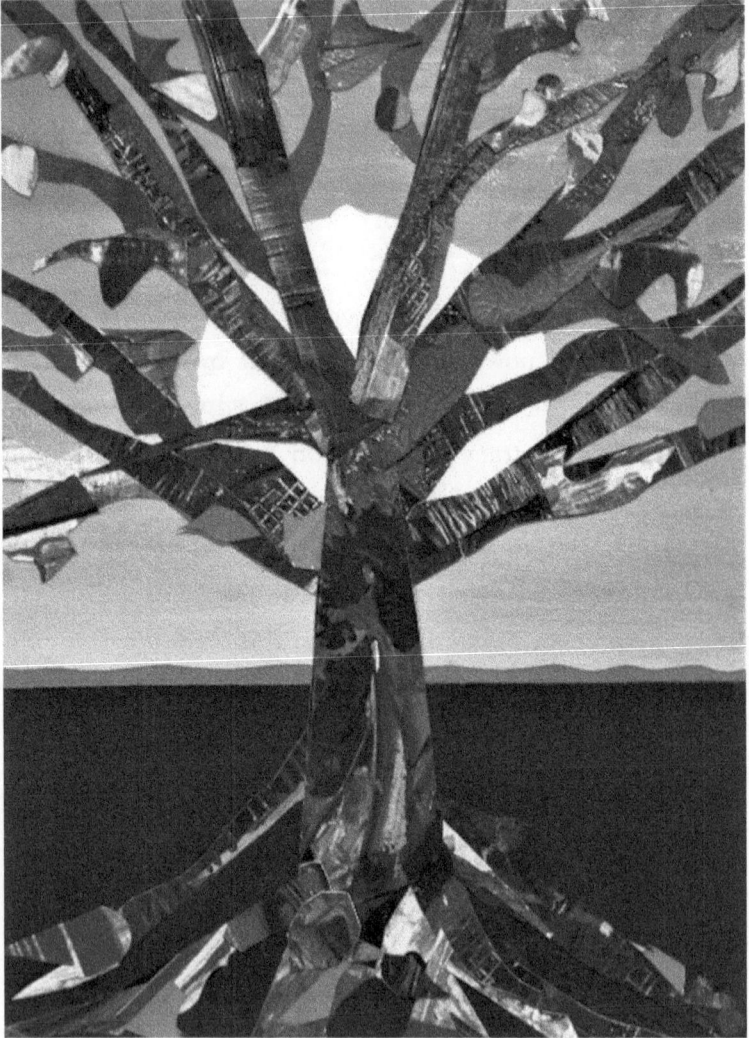

Diane: We see deep into the roots of the tree in this picture, that continue downward. They appear to be full of life and nutrients. The trunk is strong and the branches extend beyond the top of the picture. An oversized sun is rising and the hills in the far distance are minimal but beckoning.

Murray: The individuation process comes into view, from its depths in the earth to its heights reaching out of the frame to the heavens. The tree looks well-developed and strongly rooted. There is variety and complexity in the tree. One of Jung's greatest essays is titled "The Philosophical Tree." There Jung discussed the tree as the classic symbol of the individuation process, the growth of consciousness in time. The dreamer catches a glimpse of the archetypal process and its result in this image. However, this tree is much more than a personal symbol for the dreamer's life. It is huge and exceeds the boundaries of the frame. It is a world tree, like Yggdrasil, the World Tree of the Norse mythology. It connects heaven and earth and contains the whole world within is branches. It symbolizes all of humanity as a work in progress.

No. 17: The Heavenly Spiral

Diane: This picture shows an unusual relationship between a powerful bull, a young lady and a heavenly body. All three are in an intimate connection. The bull looks like Nandi, the sacred mount of the Hindu god Shiva. Nandi means "giving joy and delight." He sits solidly on four legs. The young lady is dressed simply and sits near Nandi as though they are friends. They both gaze attentively and worshipfully at the spiral of stars in the sky.

Murray: It is a meditation picture. Their eyes are fixed on the stars, which are arranged in a spiral with a bright center. The center is the transcendent Self, the source of energy and light. The feminine figure is in close and comfortable relationship with the archetypal mount of the gods. Nothing is beneath them. They are sitting quietly, contemplatively, in the Void. This picture is a snapshot taken in and of the timeless realm of eternity. As a dream image, it presents the dreamer with a symbol of what is normally invisible, the fourth (or fifth) dimension of reality. In this realm, there is no birth and no death. Everything is present at once. History does not exist as timebound in the way the ego knows it. Even astrology is surpassed because it is linked to time and movement in time of the planets, the earth, the sun and the moon. The stars in this picture symbolize eternity, not as they exist in the astronomical calculations within temporality. This is the spiritual world.

No. 18: Joining the Spirit

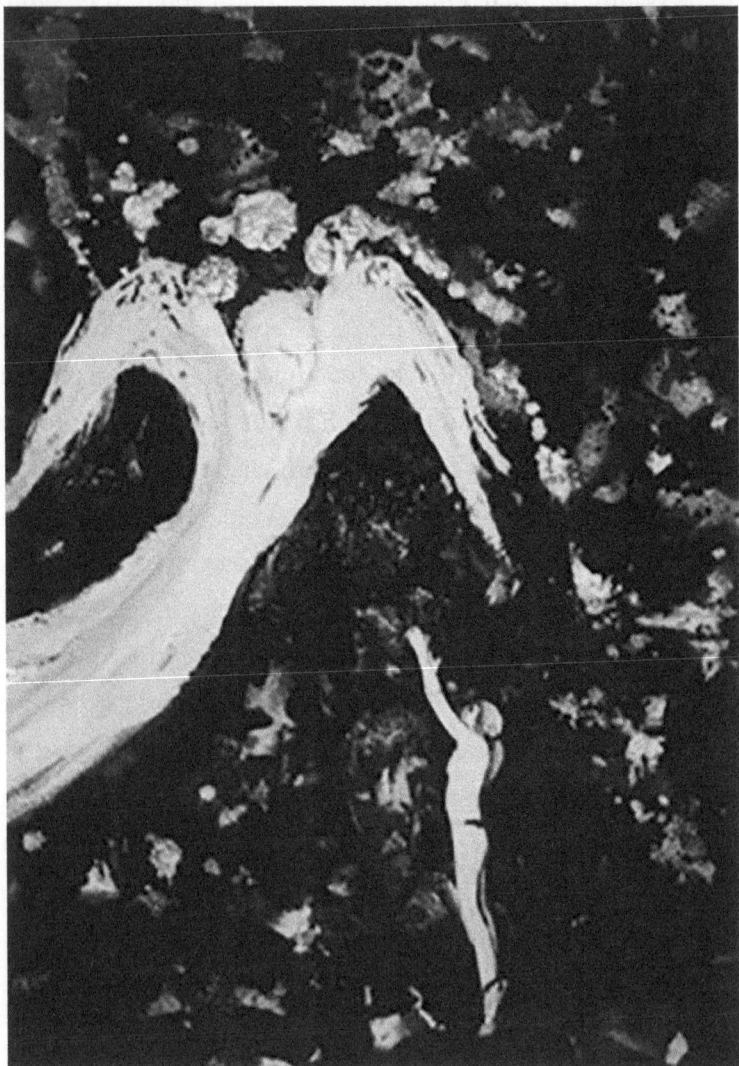

Diane: The spirit-angel looks ethereal against a black background filled with mysterious forms and shadows. The dreamer is either flying or reaching upward, clearly wishing to join with the heavenly spirit. There is clearly a relationship, but the spirit is larger, freer, and more autonomous.

Murray: It is Ascension Day! The Angel is a messenger of the Self and will carry the willing dream figure to the highest realms. This picture augers what Jung, referencing ancient Mysteries such as the Eleusinian, called "a deification mystery." The dreamer, flying upward, will be received by the magnificent spiritual messenger and taken on a journey into *unio mentalis,* and ultimately into a state of *unus mundus,* as described by Gerhard. A state of consciousness is emerging that is spiritual and reflective—not identified with people, particular places, things, or ideas. In this type of consciousness, one is able to observe and interact with others, even gurus and powerful teachers, without losing identity. The era of creating a false reality out of projections is coming to an end. This is a stage of individuation where one separates from states of identification with others and unites with the true self.

No. 19: Night Dance

Diane: We see a dancer in this picture with her head turned away from us. She is facing the stars and night sky. Her dance posture is fully stretched in an arc. This is a dance of sheer delight, filled with space and movement, yet interestingly still embodying the discipline of a trained dancer. She has not lost herself.

Murray: The dancer is celebrating her new life in the spirit. Her joy is boundless, and her body reflects her freedom to be herself spontaneously and fully. There is a feeling of play in this image, something childlike and free of inhibitions. This follows the previous picture of Ascension. In the picture, there is no sense of gravity. The laws of nature and the material world do not apply in this psychic space. This expresses the life of the soul in its own space. People who have had near death experiences (NDE's) tell of similar images and feelings. When such experiences as these are integrated and assimilated later, people show more creative ways of living and working. They are free of persona restrictions and anxieties. They have nothing to lose because their sense of value is grounded in the Self and not in others' opinions.

No. 20: Under the Moon

Diane: The dance continues! A full moon, partially covered, is reflected on the surface of the water where the dreamer is dancing. Rather than being under the sea as in #14, it's as if the sea is supporting the dreamer now. The moon, sea, and dancer are celebrating the feminine.

Murray: The lunar world is different from the solar. The light of the moon is not as strong, the differentiation of objects not as sharp, the restrictions on imagination not as tight. Here there is room for playful movement and intuitive knowing. The body is weightless and can dance on the surface of the water. Conscious and unconscious are not opposites but rather elements in a more embracing consciousness. This is what the body knows when the mind is not thinking. It is intuitive wisdom expressing itself in motion. Imagination rules in this realm. There is also an element of performance in this picture. The dancer is looking at the viewers as though wanting to show them something. Is this an invitation to join the dance? She is alone and perhaps wants a partner. Now my imagination is playing! The picture has this effect on the viewer. We want to participate imaginatively in the lunar dance.

No. 21: Returning to Earth

Diane: In this drawing the dreamer is making a great effort to pull an angel down to earth. There are actually two angels bound together, male and female. The dreamer is much larger and stronger than when she joined the spirit in picture 18. Now her gaze is not heavenward but towards the ground. It's interesting that the dreamer is completely naked and both angels are fully dressed—even to the extent of wearing jewellery and a headscarf.

Murray: The landing seems to take a considerable effort. People who experience the heights of spirituality and oneness often find it difficult to come back to everyday reality on the ground. Integration of the experience under the light of the moon is not without its challenges. The dream figure pulling the angelic couple down to earth is exerting great effort. *Unio Mentalis* is being pulled into the body. The dreamer has matured and now has the strength to pull the spirit to Earth. She is naked, without persona. The angel, on the other hand, who is both female and male, is well-defined and elegantly dressed. Their regal aspect is bound to affect the self-image of the naked dreamer when they have been brought to Earth. In her nakedness, she is open to the influence of the archetypal couple. A new persona will emerge in the future, something royal and angelic. This seems like a matured version of the young couple in Picture 8. There will be an opportunity now to live this union as embodied in time and space, and in community with others.

No. 22: Badger

Diane: A friendly badger fills the picture and is looking up at the dreamer with questioning eyes. What does he want from the dreamer? It's as though he is speaking.

Murray: The badger lives a nocturnal life close to and even within the earth. He is an earthy spirit. The black-and-white coat combines the opposites, so there is a suggestion of the Self in this image. Like the angels, he is an avatar of the transcendent. This dream image, however, is well-grounded and continues the theme of descent to body and earth that we have seen in the preceding picture. Badgers are known as fierce fighters and deep diggers. The dream image suggests an invitation to communicate with this symbol. So different from the angels in the previous pictures in one sense, the badger is however yet another avatar, a symbol that can provide a link to psychic energies of the unconscious. This image would suggest a strong instinct for self-protection, for creating alliances for mutually guarded safety zones with security measures in place, and for deep digging in search of nourishment. Like the dancer in a picture before, the badger is at home in the light of the moon.

No. 23: The Knot of Eternity

Diane: What immediately captures my attention in this picture are the coils around the center. The dreamer can't find where the knot begins or ends. The design seems to emerge from its background, as though the darkness created it. I think it's more powerful coming out of the dark than if it was broad daylight.

Murray: What a different picture from the preceding ones! This picture is geometric and abstract. This would suggest a thinking function has come into play. The pattern is an intricate mandala intersected by four strong arms in the form of a cross. The picture feels religious. Horizontal and vertical arms are centered by a circle of interwoven threads around a luminous point. The midpoint of the mandala is indivisible. It is timeless and transcendent. This beautiful dream image of wholeness brings a stabilizing symbol for the dreamer's psyche. The dynamic movements that have been flowing in the previous images here come to a halt in a highly developed and structured image of totality and wholeness. One has the feeling that this symbol is meant to serve the dreamer as a talisman and a reminder of the process imaged in the whole series of pictures. This is a culmination.

No. 24: The Pregnant Enso

Diane: I always find this painting fascinating. What is all the movement inside the circle? It reminds me of the pregnant salmon in the first picture of analysis. It's pregnant with endless possibilities. We see a white and black background in equal proportion, with an interesting, variegated square framing it. The painting does not look finished, but somehow it looks complete; the end of a process.

Murray: A circle contained in a square and backed on left and right by wings, the image emits a feeling of both dynamic movement and stability. The angels are suggested by the wings, so they remain ever present. This picture wraps up the analysis and is in the manner of fond farewell to the analyst and the project. It has been completed. In the previous picture, we witnessed the product of the individuation process. Here we find a further symbol of the Self as all-containing but replete with energy and further potential. It is fairly bursting with emergent contents. It appears pregnant and ready to give birth to new life. Analysis concludes as a prologue to further individuation.

CONVERSATION FOUR

Of Two Minds in One

Murray: Let's begin this conversation with a key question, Diane. A theme throughout our conversations has been "liberation," and we have discussed it from several angles. Now I'd like us to think about the question of the difference between what's called the dualistic mind and the non-dualistic mind. The dualistic is the I-Thou or I-It mindset based on a clear distinction between self and others. This is the normal state of consciousness for most people. It is what we call ego-consciousness. Its basic characteristic is that it makes distinctions and differentiates this from that. The ego is called the "reality tester." This refers to both material and mental realities—things as well as feelings and ideas. But there is a lot of discussion today among psychologists, philosophers and meditators about the experience of "oneness," or non-duality as it's called, and how this is missing from modernity as we refer to our times. Modernity is entirely based on ego-consciousness and on a materialistic and body-oriented rationalistic philosophy. The absence of transcendence and spirituality has become very much part of the critique of modernity's one-sidedness. The East, on the other hand, has a far greater appreciation of the non-dualistic mind, as is generally thought. Now I would like to ask you as one who is a long-time practitioner of meditation based on Tibetan Buddhism: What has the experience of non-duality been like for you? Can you describe it?

Diane: Any answer to this question seems arrogant.

Murray: Don't worry about being arrogant. Be arrogant! (Laughter)

Diane: Well, first of all some schools make a distinction between "oneness" and "non-duality." But putting that aside, one thing I can say is that the experience of oneness and non-duality, however temporary, is infinitely more expansive and complete than ego-consciousness.

Murray: Jung talks about this in many places, as you know. I'm thinking of his late work, *Aion*. There he says that our ego-consciousness is very limited. It's an outgrowth of something far deeper, of what the alchemists called *prima materia*, which Jung would call the Self. The Self is much larger than ego-consciousness. We just have a partial view of psychic reality from the viewpoint of ego-consciousness. The experience of oneness involves somehow getting behind this and realizing experientially that ego-consciousness is partial. But what is, who is, being conscious when that happens? Is the ego still there? Jung would argue that you have to have some kind of ego-consciousness present, not necessarily as the centre of the field, but as an observer. And doesn't the experience of oneness still include observer and observed?

Diane: How would you describe the 8th Ox-herding picture (*Enso*), in relation to the question you are asking?[15]

---

[15] For a commentary to all 10 Ox-herding pictures, see M. Stein, *Minding the Self*, Ch. 15.

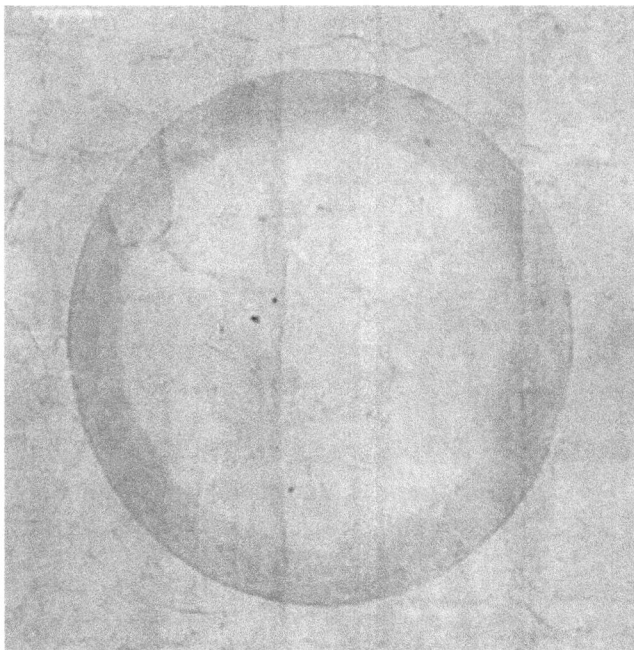

Enso – 8th Ox-herding picture[16]

Murray: I'm looking at the picture. There's an observer and the observed. If I observe the picture of the *Enso*, the circle, I'm seeing an image. If I step into that image and try to participate in the experience that image is offering, what happens? Am I seeing something, or is there no seer? I mean, this is an old, old question. I've run around this with friends in the past, and we've argued about it back and forth. Is there such a thing as an experience of oneness that has no ego in it—no observer? I'm asking about your experience.

---

[16] Ox-herding pictures by Japanese Rinzai Zen Monk Shobun, 15th century, said to be copies of originals, now lost, traditionally attributed to Kakuan, a 12th century Chinese Zen Master.

Diane: Yes, of course there is such a thing as oneness with no observer, and it has a name. It's called satori, samadhi, non-duality. But as soon as you come out of the experience, it splits. There is ego-consciousness to remember it, describe it, give it qualities, like many fingers pointing to the moon. The fingers are the descriptions, conceptual and dualistic—however finely stated. The moon is the direct experience itself.

Murray: Naming makes the realization into an "it." Wouldn't you say that many experiences are like that? Say you are in the midst of a strong emotional field. You're in love, or you're seeing a beautiful sunset. You aren't thinking about it, you're in it. Is that the same thing as non-duality?

Diane: To me it is. One day in Ireland I climbed the holy mountain, Croagh Patrick, with a few friends. It's about a 4-hour climb and gets progressively more difficult as you approach the top, where it becomes a steep ascent with loose rocks and slippery scree. You are on your hands and knees by the time you reach the peak. I guess that's part of the pilgrimage—suffering! You have to concentrate and work hard, at least we all did at our age. By the time we reached the top we were mentally and physically exhausted. You are so physically tired you can't process in the normal way and your conceptual loop just stops. That day the view was stupendous, and we all sat there in silence for an hour. Inner lucid silence. It's that feeling of mind and body falling off, and at the same time a sack is lifted from your head: *peace beyond understanding*. People report this experience often and I think it's one of the motivations

for mountain climbing, even if not known consciously.
Also, many people have numinous experiences in nature,
in love, listening to great music, etc. It's a spontaneous
experience of oneness, being totally in the moment.

Murray: Yes. So, it's not something that only advanced meditators
have. Any person climbing a mountain can have that
experience. It's pure seeing, no ego in the foreground.
No subject-object duality. I think that approaches the
meaning of the 8th Ox-herding picture, the empty circle.
What about the 9th picture? Here it is. Take a look. In
the 8th picture you are the *Enso*, the emptiness, the void,
non-duality. And then, here in the 9th picture there is no
person viewing as there was in Picture 7, but there is a

Ox-herding Picture 9: Return to the Source

scene. It's titled "Return to the Source." We have to think about the Source. What is that, psychologically speaking?

Diane: Doesn't the 9th picture refer to the foundation, the substratum? It shows the roots of a tree.

Murray: The roots are emphasized, yes.

Diane: I'm wondering if the 9th picture is a necessary step after the *Enso*, so one doesn't cling to or remain in the Void.

Murray: Yes, that's an excellent observation. Letting go of the empty mind and coming back into the temporal mind is suggested by this sequence. But this is a transitional state to the 10th picture, which shows the sage in the marketplace in conversation with a young man. In the

Ox-herding Picture 10: Entering the Market Place

sequence we see that there is a return from non-duality to everyday life and the temporal mind active in the public world. In your experience, is it a temptation to stay in the 8th picture, *Enso*?

Diane: You know it is! We all know by experience that it is a seduction to remain in that state, if only we could! (Laughter, both)

Murray: Why?

Diane: It's like being awake or conscious in deep, dreamless sleep. The seductive part is that there you have no conflict of opposites, no struggle with the shadow, no suffering the ailments of the body, no difficult relationships, no hard work to increase consciousness—in other words, a Utopian fantasy.

Murray: It can be escapist? A person can think: OK, let's dissociate permanently from the temporal mind and stay in the paradise of Oneness!

Diane: Yes, let's go where it's always sunny. (Laughter) Very idealistic. But that's not the authentic experience of *Enso,* which is rooted in the 9th and integrated in the 10th, in the marketplace.

Murray: The marketplace is your own cultural shopping mall, your hometown's Main Street. This is where you have to function as a sage. You see how emphasized the roots of the tree are in Picture 9.

Diane: I'm wondering if the last three Ox-herding pictures could be represented this way: Satori (8-Enso), rooted by the triangle (9-The Source), and completed in the square (10-Market Place). In Dzogchen we say, "View,

117

Circle-Triangle-Square

Meditation, Action." The View is direct experience of the Void (the circle). Holding the View in awareness is meditation (the triangle). The result is activity in the world, appropriate response (the square).

Murray: The three are linked and held together—three-in-one. Picture 8 is in a way the culmination of the preceding seven Ox-herding pictures. It's a high point, the mountaintop. It is then linked to the marketplace by the contact with the primal source. I like your picture. It shows the development as well as the close dependency and linkage between the two minds, the atemporal and the temporal. It also shows the state of wholeness completed in the square. The square represents the completion of the individuation process. That looks like a perfect resolution to the problem of the One and the

Many! They are integrated into a new Wholeness by love, through the heart (the triangle).

Diane: The square, or completion of the three symbols, reminds me of a passage in the "Diamond Sutra" which I will paraphrase as—after crossing the water, you don't need to drag the boat around with you.[17]

Murray: Yes. Another interesting interpretation of the picture. The boat would be the means, the techniques involved, the practices. Once wholeness has been achieved, you don't need the boat any longer.

Diane: I'm wondering if the boat might be a religion. It can save your life when the sharks are circling and assist in the crossing from potentiality to actualization, but it's not necessary when you've made the passage.

Murray: But don't you continue to practice a specific form of meditation. Why?

Diane: Because I'm not on the other shore, that's why! (Laughter) Why does a concert pianist continue practicing? Because they lose it if they don't. And it's a way of life, what makes life meaningful. I suppose for us ordinary human beings, if we don't continue going forward, we regress.

Murray: Therefore, the religious practices you learn in order to make the crossing have to continue throughout your lifetime because you remain human and subject to the division between the two minds. Being human, being in the body and in the ego, creates a handicap. We can slide back into old ego habits. We can't avoid it because

---

[17] See A.F. Price & Wong Mou-lam (tr.), *The Diamond Sutra*, Shambhala Publications, p. 23.

we have a trained brain full of memories and habits. We continue to be subject to division and splitting. The devilish shadow is never finally conquered and locked permanently in Hell.

Diane: Never locked permanently in Hell…that's funny. What do you make of the phrase, "dual-aspect monism"? Does "monism" refer to the underlying oneness beyond the divisions created by the mind?

Murray: It's a theory of oneness that says that mind and matter have a common source. I'm not sure we can experience this. We may get a glimpse of it occasionally, but it remains a hypothesis. It's behind Jung's theory of synchronicity.

Diane: How oneness is defined is important, isn't it? So-called "oneness" can be clinging to one side of a pair of opposites.

Murray: Yes, that's right. The other side is "twoness." It is better to admit both "twoness" and "oneness" than to repress one in favor of the other. The spiritualists and mystics repress "twoness"; the modern mind represses "oneness."

Diane: What about "wholeness"?

Murray: Wholeness is a condition that contains the opposites. And if wholeness contains the opposites, isn't that living with duality and non-duality at the same time?

Diane: That's my experience. Tricky, I think, to cling to one or the other. We can talk all we want about non-duality or emptiness, but you don't experience that when you smash your car into a concrete wall.

Murray: Of course. Is it possible to transcend those opposites? The word transcendent means to rise above, to the top of the mountain. You can see the opposites, but you are not divided by them. You can know them but not be possessed by them.

Diane: What do you think? In your experience as an analyst, is it possible for people to transcend the opposites?

Murray: Well, the transcendent function is something we speak about as a product of the individuation process. Jung, you know, was Swiss and he did a lot of mountain climbing for pleasure and had all kinds of experiences in the mountains. About transcendence, he says that it's like being on the mountain top and looking down into the valley. On the mountain top you are in the sunshine. Down in the valley there's a storm. With wholeness, you are in both places. You are in the storm and on the mountain top at the same time.

Diane: That's a good way to describe it.

Murray: You live with the storm in the valley, but you aren't totally consumed by it. You are also on the mountain top, but this does not remove you from the storm as would be the case if you dissociate. You are in both, and you are out of both. That's transcendence.

Diane: I wonder if psychological liberation could be this state of transcendence you describe. Here is a quote I came across in a little booklet, "Conversations with Jung" by Margaret Ostrawski-Sachs. It surprised me. "During my illness, I received confirmation and I now knew that everything had meaning and that everything was perfect. All was revealed, everything correct; everything meaningful and complete."[18]

---

[18] M. Ostrowski-Sachs, *From Conversations with C.G. Jung, Zurich:* p. 68.

Murray: Do you think he was on drugs?

Diane: He was on drugs??! Oh, that's a good one! (Laughter)

Murray: He was in the hospital, was recovering from a heart attack. It was at night. They gave him sleeping draughts because he couldn't sleep. And he woke up during the night and had these remarkable visions.

Diane: Whatever he's on, I want some. (Laughter)

Murray: It was a big experience, for sure. He speaks about it in *Memories, Dreams, Reflections* as one of the most important in his life.[19] He had sublime visions. But when he comes out of the hospital, he becomes terribly depressed. He says, "Oh, I have to return to this life." Back to the marketplace, the train station, the box of everyday life in the body and with all kinds of people.

Diane: Still, what he describes could be a description of samadhi, satori or *realization*.

Murray: There you are, but it's back to the dualistic mind. That's the nature of ego-consciousness. It creates separations, distinctions. It separates us from the objects around us, the people around us. We have what we call an identity. And then on another level we know we are all one. Sometimes we even feel that and experience that fundamental oneness. But we live in both climates. That is wholeness.

In the East, they speak of liberation from all suffering. This is discovered and then cultivated through meditation. In depth psychology, we hope for some relief from the

---

[19] See C.G. Jung, *Memories, Dreams, Reflections*, pp. 289 ff.

complexes and other controlling forces of the unconscious and eventually a union of the opposites, conscious and unconscious. What is true liberation? Is there a difference between true liberation and a mere fantasy of liberation? You mentioned that in a message to me a while back.

Diane: Well! When I was reflecting on this last night, the examples of the *fantasy of liberation* just kept coming, reams of paper. (Laughter, both) Whereas, "true liberation"—not much to say! In a nutshell, all fantasy of liberation has some degree of ego-posturing. "I'm enlightened—where is my throne?"

Murray: Oh yes. It becomes competitive and divisive.

Diane: Let me ask you, in your experience with depth psychology in general and the work with analysands in particular, what is "liberation" in a successful analysis?

Murray: I haven't used the term liberation very much until recently. It must be your influence, Diane. It's not in the psychology dictionary. It's a term that Buddhists use frequently to refer to a desired state of mind but not very often by psychoanalysts. What I see, however, is a possibility for people to experience a degree of liberation from the grip of their complexes, if they do the work in analysis. If they work on their dreams, reflect on their emotional states of mind, do active imagination, and so forth, they develop a different kind of relationship to themselves and to the world around them. They become freer. That new relationship liberates them from certain knee-jerk emotional reactions that we say are complex driven. For instance, there's a woman who had a very difficult experience with her mother, and continues to be troubled by her relationship. When she is with her mother, she feels like a child, and her mother treats her like a child. Over the years as we have worked on this, she has begun to see her mother much more clearly, more objectively. She can step out of her complex when she looks at her mother. She can see her mother as a separate human being who is struggling, who has her own history, and she can feel some compassion for her mother. I would call that liberation from the complex. It has been a long, difficult process, and she still falls back in certain moments when she is with her mother. She can regress. But then she can step out of it. One lives in two states of mind. You know, there is a liberated part of us and a not-so-liberated part of us. We move back and forth between them. The complexes are never totally dissolved. Why don't the complexes disappear? Why do they stay around? It's very strange. They should go once you analyse them. They don't because there is an archetypal core to the complex. And that archetype never goes away. It belongs to a person's humanity, to the collective unconscious. It's something we inherit as human beings. So, the mother complex, for instance, has at its core something that is permanent, the mother archetype. You can put aside the personal parts, and this offers a degree of liberation. The mother archetype at the core of the mother complex, however, is with you always. And it is different from the personal mother, from the dramatic experiences you've had with your mother. This has a purpose. The liberation that can be achieved through analysis doesn't affect these archetypal levels, nor should it.

Diane: In your book, *Outside, Inside and All Around*, you say: "In nearly all analytical cases that go deep, the result is an abiding awareness of the timeless dimension of the soul. This experience is the much sought-after treasure hard to obtain."[20]

Murray: Yes. And the experience of the archetypal mother is one of those. Goethe writes famously in *Faust* Part Two of the "descent to the mothers." This was important for Faust's individuation. It's the descent to the depths of the unconscious, a part of the individuation journey.

Diane: Even if one is able to experience that, it's not a permanent experience, is it? Our minds and bodies go through continual change. But when you have had a definite and felt experience of the *timeless dimension of the soul*, your confidence is continuous.

Murray: Yes, that confidence is based on experience and not on a theory. That's what is so important. I think active imagination is so important for individuation.

Diane: Murray, you often emphasize how valuable active imagination is. I know eight people who have done Jungian analysis in the last ten years. None of them were introduced to active imagination and don't know what it is. I've been to dozens of lectures at Jungian clubs as well as countless Jungian lectures online, and a presentation of Active Imagination is extremely rare. Do you have any idea why this is? Has it fallen off the Jungian table?

---

[20] M. Stein, *Outside, Inside and All Around*, p.101-102.

Murray: I'm afraid it has, sadly. But it's made a comeback since the publication of *The Red Book* in 2009. This got people's attention. For Jung, active imagination was the Royal Road to individuation. Without it, it's not possible to arrive at the destination. When teachings get institutionalized, they always lose something of the original genius and spirit of the visionary founder. This has happened in Analytical Psychology as well.

Diane: A few people I've met who are not in Jungian analysis but have studied extensively, such as Jung's *Red Book*, *Memories, Dreams, Reflections* and so forth, have expressed interest in doing active imagination. I don't know what to tell them. Is there a danger that without being in formal analysis it could turn into daydreaming?

Murray: Not really. But if a person has unstable psychic foundations, it could trigger a psychosis, which means losing a sense of reality for a period of time and becoming identified with unconscious energies and images. It's best to have the guidance of an analyst or someone schooled and familiar with the various problems that can arise. The unconscious isn't really something to play around with. It's not a parlor game.

Diane: Does active imagination remain a valuable resource even after decades of experience, such as in your own life?

Murray: Absolutely! It's an essential part of my life. It's an ongoing practice, like yoga and meditation are for you.

Diane: And I have one final question on the subject. Artists like Jackson Pollack did Jungian analysis. Contemporary artists, especially abstract expressionists, seem to be in creative dialogue with the unconscious when they paint. Is that active imagination?

Murray: I don't know. I'd have to speak with them about it. Do they have conversations with the images? That is an essential aspect of active imagination. It's a dialogue. By conversation, I don't necessarily mean talking in words, but rather communicating back and forth, ideas, viewpoints, attitudes. That sort of thing. It's two-way.

Diane: In my experience, active imagination is so important in making the unconscious visible through images and paintings. It's making dreams and inner figures come alive with form and color. It gives one more independence, doesn't it?

Murray: Yes, it's a way of extending and expanding the experience of the inner world. When you have a sense of the other world within, it can offer guidance and intuitive wisdom. So that extends the range of independence from outer authorities.

Diane: With such an experience, there's not so much tension between the opposites: it's more of a marriage. The temporal needs the timeless, and the timeless needs the temporal. They are not in a battle. They are in a very meaningful and purposeful relationship.

Murray: Exactly! They come together in the psyche. We call this integration. The two minds become one. And this seems a good place to stop!

CONVERSATION FIVE

Liberation: Limits and Prospects

Diane: We began by discussing the notion of liberation—both spiritual and psychological. Now I would like to ask if you think liberation is even possible, given our conditioning. Here is a quote from Jung:

> He has only to realize that he is shut up
> inside his mind and cannot step beyond it,
> even in insanity; and that the appearance of
> his world or of his gods very much depends
> upon his own mental condition.[21]

As Jung says here, our perception depends on our mental condition with all its habits and consuming thought patterns. Perhaps we are always seeing through glass darkly, or like the people in the cave Plato describes we are only looking at projections but not seeing the origin of the projections. Can numinous experience liberate us from this state of unconsciousness, from our habitual concepts and assumptions? What is liberation in depth psychology?

---

[21] C. G. Jung, "Psychological Commentary on *The Tibetan Book of the Great Liberation.*" *Collected Works*, vol. 11, para. 765.

Murray: Truth is, depth psychology says that numinous images are also projections. In other words, the question is: are we forever trapped within our psyches? Is there no liberation from this condition? Let me speak first from my experience as a Jungian psychoanalyst. We work with individuals, and the individual comes with a history. In analysis we look at that history, we examine that history carefully. We try to analyse it and to find repeating patterns in it. In doing that, consciousness emerges that is able to look at that history more objectively. We are less embedded in it than before. We use various concepts to analyse the patterns. For instance, we speak of complexes and cultural and archetypal patterns. The purpose of all of this is to get a more objective view of our lives and our relationships to others, beginning with the earliest relationships in our families. We spend quite a lot of time looking at early history and childhood. Some measure of liberation comes from this. But from my experience—and I think any analyst who has worked for any length of time will testify, as Jung also did—you don't ever completely liberate yourself from the effects of the complexes that were developed during your early history. They are always crouching at the door waiting to spring on you, given a suitable provocation. It would be an illusion, from a Jungian perspective, to say that we can ever be liberated from our history and our complexes in the sense that we would never, ever, see them again or experience their emotional effects on us. I have worked with people who have had a huge amount of experience in analysis and various forms of religious life—whether Eastern or Western, meditation or prayer, and so on—and without exception they will occasionally get caught up in what we call *complex discharging*. These are situations where some cue sets off a strong emotional reaction and they lose control over themselves and do and say things that in retrospect they see very clearly are the effects of a discharge of energy from complexes.

Your question reaches out for another possibility. If we have numinous experiences, is it possible to decrease the power of complexes and increase the factor of liberation? Does numinous experience help with liberation from complexes and habitual patterns of thinking and feeling? Again, from my experience and talking to other Jungian analysts and students, as well as with people who come from other theoretical perspectives, I would say that numinous experience can help but only if it is worked with further. By itself, it creates a momentary lift out of the historical into the transcendent, where we have the feeling of liberation and we see the big picture, the reality behind the obvious persuasions of the senses and our normal patterns of thinking. But this does not last very long, unless it is worked with further. The experience itself is only a first step toward another stage or degree of what one could call freedom or liberation from conditioning.

What we have been taught as Jungian analysts, and experienced in our own work, and what we can read about in Jung's *Collected Works* and *The Red Book* and so on, is that by working with the numinous experience, taking it further and using it as a kind of reference point or North Star to orient ourselves when we're caught up again in the everyday world of temporality and the ego, it can remind us of, and even bring us back into, that state of mind that we could call more liberated. Then we can take it further, step by step. That is what the individuation process is, step by step. The transcendent function is where one has a bigger perspective. As Jung describes it, there's a storm in the valley but one can see it from the mountain top as well as being in the storm at the same time. That describes this experience of being in the complexes and yet also knowing it at the same time from another perspective. That is an extent of liberation that can be achieved by the type of work that we do in analysis.

Without numinous experience, it is probably not possible to take those further steps. Without it, you could get bogged down with the same analysis of the same complexes over and over again. That's the reason Jung left the Freudian way of working. He said if you just rely on free association to dream material, you repeat over and over again the same patterns of thought. You never get out of your thought patterns; you simply deepen them. There is that danger in some psychotherapies, that they simply repeat the narratives, which in fact deepens the neurosis. By repeating it, the patterns of thinking and feeling become more entrenched in the psyche. Even though the therapist has good intentions, empathizing and mirroring, this isn't sufficient to actually step out of the conditioning. It needs something else, and for that we rely on these extraordinary experiences in dreams and active imagination, which give us that first step toward arriving at the transcendent function.

That is a long-winded response to your very important question, is liberation possible? I think one can over-emphasize the possibility. There is such a thing as illusory liberation. People suppose that they are liberated, but if you look at their actual lives you quickly find that they are not liberated from their complexes. Of course, there are also people who completely dismiss the possibility and say there is absolutely no way one can break out of conditioning: One just has to settle into it, make the best of it, and try to minimize the effects as much as possible from a rational point of view. I try to walk a middle path between overly optimistic and overly pessimistic. I think there is a possibility, but one has to go slowly, step by step. Even the smallest degree of liberation is a product of a lot of work, and, in fact, the project of achieving liberation from the psyche's engrained patterns is never-ending. One doesn't ever get completely liberated.

Diane: Excellent, Murray. Thank you. So, when Zen Master Hiramatsu asked Jung if we can ever be free from the collective unconscious, and Jung answered "Yes," that might have been a bit of a joke?

Murray: I think Jung was drawn down a path of ascent by a very clever Zen Master. Master Hiramatsu asked him if one can be liberated from complexes, and Jung responded that, yes, to some degree that is possible. Then he asked, what about archetypes? Can a person also be liberated from their influence? Jung thought for a moment, and affirmed that yes, to an extent that is possible. And what about the collective unconscious? Jung seemed to think slowly and suddenly said, yes, that too. We don't know what he was considering in that moment. Perhaps he was recalling some experiences of transcendence he had in the course of his long life. Hiramatsu was satisfied and ended the conversation at that point, seeing that Jung was tired. They had been using the word "self" and "true self" to refer to this type of liberation and transcendence, and in retrospect Jung wanted to take back what he said. He realized that they had not worked out carefully enough the meaning of the terms they were using.

I do believe that moments of such total liberation are possible, and that Jung himself did have that experience. Jung was old and physically weak at the time of that interview. He was two years or so from his death. He had had a lot of amazing psychological experiences. Among these was a release from temporality into a space where nothing really matters, where there are no longer the effects of gravity. He tells Aniela Jaffé about such visionary experiences, and she recorded them in *Memories, Dreams, Reflections*. I'm thinking especially about an experience he reports that occurred while he was in the hospital in 1944 with a heart attack. During the night, and for several nights, he had powerful visions. He said they were the most extraordinary and wonderful experiences he ever had in his life. In one of them, he was beyond the earth and going toward a place where he would have all his questions answered. He was free of gravity. And he also experienced visions of the hierosgamos, the sacred marriage. Everything was coming together beautifully. And then he returned to his hospital bed. "Now gray morning is coming again, now comes the gray world with its boxes! What idiocy, what hideous nonsense."[22] These are his feelings upon returning to normal consciousness. Now he had to go home and face everyday life again. The complexes and patterns were not permanently overcome.

Coming back from trips like that, from the mountain top into the valley of everyday life can be a real shock. You, Diane, have experienced it, and to an extent so have I. Many people experience liberation in various contexts, but it's not sustainable permanently. One can remember it, one can honour it, one can use it as a reference point, a North Star, but one does continue living in the temporal world and in the body. And in the body life becomes more difficult as you get older. You can't take the body for granted as you used to. Things go wrong. You are surprised by frailties that you never expected would come. Living in the body takes up an enormous amount of time and energy, focus and attention. And that is a real challenge to the transcendence from temporality, the life in the spirit on the mountain top. One has to take care of the body, and politics, and the climate, and economics. All of that, which we are bedevilled by and have to take seriously and have to deal with. That's why I think Jung

---

[22] C.G. Jung, *Memories, Dreams, Reflections*, p. 295.

wanted to take that back as a final answer. Yes, you can have this experience on occasion. And you can remember it and honour it, but it's not a permanent state of mind.

Of course, as you well know, in some cultures this type of transcendence is really cultivated. Provisions are made to support it. We don't have that so much in our modern cultures. We still have some monasteries, but we don't have the kind of cultural support you would have in India or old Tibet. There the cultures honour these states of mind and people contribute to their sustenance. It was the same in Europe in the Middle Ages. One could withdraw into a monastery and retreat entirely and permanently while being supported materially and culturally. But, you know, even there, people still lived with their complexes, their problems, their emotional conditions. The conflicts among the brothers and sisters were also acute at times. There was rivalry, resentment, unfair preference. You see this in the biblical stories of Jesus and his disciples. Who comes first? Who gets to sit beside him in the Kingdom to come? Who is the closest? Who is the favoured one? Even among the saints there are these types of problems. They aren't liberated totally and permanently. The ego is still present and active, insistent on its priority.

Diane: While we humans long for the timeless and transcendent, the spirit realm might long for the particular and limited.

Murray: It's a pair of opposites, the temporal and the non-temporal. And when you are dealing with opposites, there is always the danger of going to an extreme in one direction or the other, either to the material or to the spiritual. There may be a sudden reversal, which is what Heraclitus called enantiodromia. You go so far into spirituality, and then there is a sudden reversal into gross instinctuality, and then perhaps you try to swing back into the spiritual extreme after making a confession of sin. The reversal of the opposites is what we try to avoid in analysis. We try to hold the opposites, to respect both sides. To hold the tension of the opposites is painful. You have to experience both sides, but not overly identify with either one of them, then walk a middle path that recognizes both. Sometimes you lean more in one direction, and sometimes more in the other.

That's the concept of wholeness that we work with. Wholeness includes everything that is in the psyche: the complexes, instincts, archetypal patterns, the personal and cultural history. It also includes the non-temporal, the spiritual, transcendent. One tries to live in recognition of all of that. That might sound wishy-washy or indecisive. As my father-in-law said, "Pick a lane, any lane, just pick a lane. Don't drive all over the road." We try to drive down the middle and avoid enantiodromia. Sometimes this involves swerving. What holding to one side all the time does is create shadow. The shadow is the neglected, the unlived, the repressed, the rejected, but it doesn't go away. That's the problem. If it would go away permanently, you wouldn't have enantiodromia. But the instincts don't go away, nor does the spirit. The body doesn't go away, as long as you are living in the body, and the spirit also does not vanish. There are people who live a life of the flesh, who live totally for pleasure, sensual enjoyment and satisfaction, comfort. But there is also a terrible hunger for spirit, which is mostly unacknowledged.

Western culture nowadays is so much oriented toward the body and material well-being—food, health, longevity, lack of pain and suffering, comfort, and without much explicit reference to the spiritual. Because of this we have the strange compensatory phenomenon of the pop-up meditation centers in shopping malls. People who are shopping in the malls, totally oriented to the material ("What's new? What's the latest? What's the cheapest?"), suddenly register a hunger for something else, and they step into the pop-up meditation center where they can experience tranquillity, another kind of pleasure that can't be found in the shops. The more dedicated you are to shopping in the mall, the stronger this hunger gets because it isn't being lived. On the other hand, if you are living in the monastery, you will develop a very strong hunger for what the shadow world has to offer in its bars, nightclubs, restaurants, pleasure palaces. You will be fascinated by them and lose yourself in them for a while.

So, the middle way is not really an indefinite way, or a way to avoid making choices. It's an attempt to find a way to live one's wholeness in such a way that the other side of whatever opposites there are isn't totally lost sight of, neglected and repressed.

There's an amusing scene in Jung's *Red Book* where he is in a kitchen and speaking with an old cook about *The Imitation of Christ,* a famous medieval book by Thomas a Kempis,[23] when suddenly some spirits of the dead come rushing in. They are unhappy and cannot find rest. They don't know what they have done wrong, where they should go, or how they can find a resolution to their problems. So, they are going to go to Jerusalem to pray in the holy places. They are Anabaptists, people who live for the spirit alone. The leader asks Jung if he knows their mistake. What did they not live enough? he asks. Jung answers that he did not live his animal. That's where their problem lies. It isn't that they need more spirituality, which is what they will find in Jerusalem. They haven't lived the animal enough. The animal, our instinctual side—pleasure, eating, sexuality, sensuality, beauty, aesthetics, all of that—is part of our nature as animals, as members of the human species of mammals. We need to recognize that and keep it in mind even when we practice spirituality. I think you make a good job of it, Diane. You are very aesthetically oriented, you enjoy good things, and you certainly don't neglect the spiritual, nor the personal, the historical, the people around you, your relationships. You keep track of both sides. I think that's the way to go forward with individuation.

Diane: As you were speaking, I was thinking of a definition for psychological and spiritual liberation: Liberating the Self from its hidden condition in the Unconscious. Does that work?

---

[23] See C.G. Jung, *The Red Book*, Reader's Edition, pp. 334ff.

Interior

Murray: Yes, I like that. The Self can be liberated more and more. This is what Jung speaks about as the result of his mystical experiences. He was able to affirm his destiny, as he says, and to accept reality as it is without turning away from any aspect of it.[24] That's individuation. In the picture, that looks like a luminous Pearl in the dark depths.

Diane: It does look like a pearl. The pearl of great price is sometimes a symbol of the Self, isn't it? I recently had painful dental surgery. Psychologically, during and after, I felt certain that the most important thing in human life, the priceless pearl, is love and human kindness. In a normal state that sounds trite and simplistic, an embarrassing thing to say or hear. But in a vulnerable state everything is stripped away.

Murray: To me, it does not sound trite to say that love is the pearl of great price.

Diane: I often contemplate what you said in our first conversation: "Love never fails." I notice that it deeply changes one's outlook in almost any situation. I have one more follow-up question for today's discussion.

Murray: Yes?

Diane: What distinguishes—I won't use the word liberation anymore, I will say wholeness—what qualities distinguish wholeness from the unexamined life? D.T. Suzuki in *Zen Buddhism and Psychoanalysis* states:

---

[24] C.G. Jung, *Memories, Dreams, Reflections*, pp. 297-98.

From the Zen point of view, what uniquely,
psychologically distinguishes the experience
of the self is that it is saturated with the feeling
of autonomy, freedom, self-determination,
and lastly creativity. [25]

Are these four qualities (autonomy, freedom, self-determination, and creativity) signs of an individuated personality?

Murray: The unexamined life is the normal state of mind people live with. Much is left unconscious. Of the four qualities Suzuki lists, I think three of them—autonomy, freedom and self-determination—seem to speak of this level of ego functioning. On the one hand, there is a kind of illusory sense of autonomy, freedom and self-determination. If you look at small children two and three years old, they are coming into a stage of ego development that grasps for autonomy. They begin to have a will of their own. They want to do something when they want to do it and how they want to do it. I remember my son going to the refrigerator, opening it and screaming, "I want that ice cream now!" I said, "No. You have to wait until dessert time." "No! I want it now!" He was about two or three years old. He grabbed for it, and I had to hold him back. So, he didn't have full autonomy and I wasn't willing to give it to him. That insistence on autonomy is an ego wish. Is the ego really autonomous, free and self-determining? From a psychological point of view, the

[25] See D. T. Suzuki, E. Fromm, R. De Martino, *Zen Buddhism and Psycho-analysis*, p. 30.

ego is always under the influence of something beyond itself—parents, peers, instincts, complexes. So, what is real autonomy, freedom and self-determination? It is self-agency. When the ego is aligned with the Self, this becomes possible. One is no longer controlled by external forces or influences. Unfortunately, the people that are shouting loudest about autonomy, freedom and self-determination these days are intending something else. They are often politically right-wing nationalists. They want freedom for their party and captivity for everyone else. I think one has to be careful with these terms. True autonomy, freedom and self-determination is something other.

At the more developed stages of individuation, the ego gives itself over to the Self and accepts that the Self ultimately determines the fundamental direction of one's life. You can call this "destiny." Everyone has a specific destiny. The isolated, cut-off ego's sense of freedom is largely illusory. We think we have free choice when we are actually following the crowd mentality. The conditioning and teachings have been inculcated into us and cemented into our neurons, and while we may think we are free and self-determining we actually are not. Ultimately, what determines our destiny is not the ego's so-called free choices. If we become conscious of this, we begin to pay attention to what the Self is up to. That means, for instance, when a synchronicity happens one takes notice of it, extracts the meaning from it, and follows up on the meaning. You can ignore the meaning and say, "That's just a curiosity and an accident and doesn't mean anything." But if you are open to the direction of the Self, you will look more closely at the synchronicity and ask, "What's the meaning in it?" And then, when you discover the meaning, you may follow the meaning and take some steps in the direction the meaning suggests. In that way, the Self guides and determines the direction and the ego cooperates. The ego is servant of the Self. That sense of self-determination would be very much in line with what we speak of as cooperating with the individuation that is happening within you. It's going on. The program is running. You can fight it, ignore it, be unconscious of it, or you could cooperate with it. If you cooperate with it, your life has much more meaning. You have a sense of destiny. You are following a course that has been laid down for you in the timeless realm of the Self.

The last item on Suzuki's list, "creativity," is one of the five that Jung includes in his list of "instincts."[26] The instincts are a mystery. They are more than biological drives. There are different levels and expressions of the instincts, including creativity. There is the kind of shallow, tricky creativity that people use in advertising or creating slogans, logos, and so on, basically trying to manipulate people. I'm pretty sure artificial intelligence will have this ability as well. It's creativity of a type, but there is a deep creativity that is a mystery. It isn't just cleverness or a talented brain. If you look at the great creators of art like Mozart or Bach, Dante or Shakespeare, there's a profound

---

[26] C.G. Jung, "Psychological Factors Determining Human Behavior," *Collected Works*, vol. 8, paras. 237-245.

mystery to their creativity. Where does this come from? Yes, they are surrounded by traditions in music, they use tunes and ideas from other sources, they are playing with the same instruments, and they are embedded in a particular moment of culture. AI has as much. But there is something more to their creativity.

I once worked in analysis with a professional musician who played at a very important level in a first-tier orchestra. He would occasionally try to compose a piece of music. He was a very good musician, could play his instrument perfectly, and was always playing other people's music. But when he tried to write some for himself, he just couldn't do it. He told me, "There's something about Mozart. It's like he has a key to a set of drawers that are locked. He turns the key and takes out what is in the drawer—divine music! He has the key, I don't."

That key is the link to creativity in its depths. It taps into the Self. It's Mozart's "genius." It's not his ego's creation. He was given that key. He didn't learn it. He just came into the world with it in his hands. It opens the door to the Source, to the musical spirit, which is endlessly creative. It's the Self, the source of light. It's the eternal flame. Some people have that key. Mozart's father was also a musician and wrote some nice pieces, but he didn't have the genius, the key, that his son had. Nor did the children of Bach, though they were good musicians and wrote nice pieces of music, but they were copying. Imitation is the way of the ego; creativity is the way of the

Self. Bach's children were good imitators, but they weren't originals. The originals are a mystery. They come with a gift in their hands, and the best we can do is recognize them and thank them for their works because they leave us with treasures.

I think Jung had access to the Source, and it shows in his works, especially in the Red Book and in his late writings on alchemical symbols. In Jungian studies these days, scholars are locating various influences on Jung. There were a lot of them. He read widely: Schopenhauer, Kant, Nietzsche, Freud, William James, on and on. The list is long. He drank deeply from many cisterns, but his originality wasn't sourced in his library. It came from somewhere else, from the Self. That's what makes him an original. He could have been a good Freudian like Franz Alexander or Karl Abraham, maybe with some extra Swiss colours but basically true to the Master. Freud was also a genius. He came up with original ideas, but he was more tied to his times than Jung was. Jung transcended it, or some part of him did, so that he could go to the wellspring, dip deeply into it and bring out the water of life, which we are still drinking. I think he will be read through the ages because of that. His writings will not fade. Not all of his writings are on that high level, but the great ones are.

That type of creativity depends on being liberated from the ego's narrow boundaries and the spirit of the times. If you have the key to that type of liberation and can use it to open the drawers fixed to the high walls of the Self, and let come into you what is there, to make itself known, then you too will experience that level of creativity. People will notice that you are different—that you have something special, something extra that is difficult to account for on the basis of your background, studies and cultural background.

Diane: Thank you for that inspiring and thorough answer to D.T. Suzuki. Before we wind up our five conversations on Ways to the Self, I would like to offer a drawing while remembering Jung's shocking statement that he would rather be whole than enlightened!

Unus Mundus

Murray: As I look at the picture, Diane, I see a mandala with a highly energized center radiating beams outward. Stability and balance are features that strike the eye. The nuclear center is the source of energy. The rays from the nucleus shine powerfully outward into the surrounding areas in all four directions. The nucleus is contained in a larger circle, which shows the complex ingredients of the personality, potentials for future developments. I can see it as a picture of the original Self, the God within. The circles are protected by four strong bars, two light and two dark, a pair of opposites that are penetrated by the light of the Self. The two on the right and left might be defenses of the Self, structures that shield the inner personality from intrusion on both sides, conscious and unconscious. The two arranged on the vertical axis are light and allow for entry of images from the worlds above and below. It's a picture of stable and protected wholeness. Jung wrote about this type of image: "…symbols of wholeness… are usually quaternary and consist of two pairs of opposites … left/right, above/below. The four points demarcate a circle, which, apart from the point itself, is the simplest symbol of wholeness and therefore the simplest God-image."[27]

Diane: Perhaps this integration and wholeness is attainable, or if not completely attainable in our lifetime, it can give our lives inspiration and meaning. Speaking of inspiration and meaning, last night I finished reading your *Collected*

---

[27] C.G. Jung, "The Philosophical Tree," *Collected Works*, vol. 13, paras. 456-7.

Writings, Vol. 8: *Psychology and Spirituality.* I have read all the published volumes of your *Collected Writings* now. Despite my spiritual bias, or perhaps because of it, I was moved by this volume the most. It's a classic that can be placed next to any Eastern classics, ancient and modern. I was wondering why? Behind the erudite and beautiful passages is obviously an author who has gone far towards integrating the timeless and temporal, the spiritual and psychological. I will treasure it. Now that you are 80 years old, you are immune to ego-inflation and praise so I can freely express myself! Thank you, Murray, for taking part in these Five Conversations. I have greatly enjoyed it.

Murray: I thank you, Diane, for your companionship of this journey. It has been a joy for me to speak with you about ways to the Self.

References

Jung, C.G. (1937/1969). "Psychological Factors Determining Human Behavior." *Collected Works*, vol. 8. Princeton, NJ: Princeton University Press.

_____. (1951/1968). *Aion. Collected Works*, vol. 9ii. Princeton, NJ: Princeton University Press.

_____. (1954/1967). "The Philosophical Tree," *Collected Works*, vol. 13. Princeton, NJ: Princeton University Press.

_____. (1954/1969). "'Psychological Commentary' on *The Tibetan Book of the Great Liberation*." *Collected Works*, vol. 11. Princeton, NJ: Princeton University Press.

_____. (1961). *Memories, Dreams, Reflections*. Recorded and edited by Aniela Jaffé. New York: Vintage Books.

_____. (2009). *The Red Book: Liber Novus. A Reader's Edition*. New York: W. W. Norton.

Molino, A. (ed.). (1998). "The Jung-Hisamatsu Conversation" in *The Couch and the Tree*. London: Open Gate Press.

Ostrowski-Sachs, M. (1971). *From Conversations with C.G. Jung, Zurich*. Zurich: Juris Druck & Verlag.

Price, A.F., Wong Mou-lam (tr.). (1990). *The Diamond Sutra*. Boulder, CO: Shambhala Publications.

Stein, M. (2014). "Not Just a Butterfly," in *Minding the Self*. East Sussex, U.K. & New York: Routledge.

_____. (2014). "Minding the Self," in *Minding the Self*, ch.15. East Sussex, U.K., New York: Routledge.

_____. (2017). *Outside, Inside and All Around.* Asheville, NC: Chiron Publications.

_____. (2019). "Psychological Individuation and Spiritual Enlightenment," in *Collected Writings* Vol.1. Asheville, NC: Chiron Publications.

_____. (2022), "The Mystery of Transcendence – A Dream for Our Time," in *The Mystery of Transformation.* Asheville, NC: Chiron Publications.

_____. (2024). *Psychology and Spirituality,* in *Collected Writings,* vol 8. Asheville, NC.: Chiron Publications.

Suzuki, D.T., Fromm, E, De Martino, R. (1960). *Zen Buddhism and Psychoanalysis.* New York, USA: Harper & Row.

Biographies

Murray Stein is a graduate of Yale University (B.A. and M.Div.), the University of Chicago (PhD.), and the C.G. Jung Institut-Zurich (Diploma). He has been the President of the International Association for Analytical Psychology (2001-2004) and of the International School of Analytical Psychology-Zurich (2008-2012). He is the author of many books including *Jung's Map of the Soul, Four Pillars of Jungian Psychoanalysis, Men Under Construction* and *The Mystery of Transformation*. Eight volumes of his *Collected Writings* have been published to date.

Diane Stanley is a graduate of the University of Colorado in Boulder (B.A.) in Comparative World Religions and holds a diploma from a 3-year arts school in Switzerland (École de Vitrail et Création), following which she worked in a private art gallery in central London for over ten years, specializing in classical European and Asian art. She practiced and studied Buddhist meditation intensively for over four decades, both in the West and East, while also completing a Jungian analysis in the U.K.

www.ingramcontent.com/pod-product-compliance
Lightning Source LLC
Chambersburg PA
CBHW020706270326
41928CB00005B/292